T0196040

I have known Dr. Eric Evenhuis for over 10 years. In the last three years, I have had the honor to get to know him more deeply through his service as a member of our Chaplaincy and Care Ministry's Advisory Council. Dr. Evenhuis has the gift of extending hospitality to all people. His expertise on providing pastoral counseling, generous heart to serve others, and wonderful sense of humor have been a true blessing to our 150 chaplains, our ministry, and our Christian Reformed Denomination.

Rev. Sarah Roelofs, BCC, Endorser
Director of Chaplaincy & Care Ministry
Christian Reformed Church in North America

Eric Evenhuis was one of my Clinical Pastoral Education stand-outs at Pine Rest Christian Mental Health Center. He continues to help wounded souls recover and thrive. His life story has significantly equipped him to be a healer and encourager. He is a bright light in our world.

Dr. James Kok
Bellflower, CA

Dr. Eric Evenhuis first came to my attention at a clinical conference in Kansas City. At the time I was searching for a chaplain to serve at our psychiatric clinic. We wanted a "man of the cloth" with a deep personal faith, a man with full academic credentials, and a loving, caring personality. Eric fit the bill. With a warm handshake, we began a lifetime of professional and personal friendship. A fortuitous blessing was the addition of his gifted and charming wife, Nancy. His book is a gem.

Gary J. Voorman M.D.,
Founder and Director of The Voorman Psiatric Clinic, Ret.

Little Ricky's Circle of Trust

The Life and Times of Eric Evenhuis

ERIC FRANZ EVENHUIS D.MIN.

WESTBOW
PRESS®
A DIVISION OF THOMAS NELSON
& ZONDERVAN

WestBow Press books may be ordered through booksellers or by contacting:

WestBow Press
A Division of Thomas Nelson & Zondervan
1663 Liberty Drive
Bloomington, IN 47403
www.westbowpress.com
844-714-3454

ISBN: 978-1-6642-0468-3 (sc)
ISBN: 978-1-6642-0470-6 (hc)
ISBN: 978-1-6642-0469-0 (e)

Library of Congress Control Number: 2020917144

Print information available on the last page.

WestBow Press rev. date: 09/25/2020

Contents

Introduction

Do not forget to entertain strangers, for
by doing, some people have entertained
angels without knowing it.
—Hebrews 13:2 (NIV)

I own a marvelous 1993 Mercedes AMG with only 35,000 miles. I call it the "Presidential Limousine." Nevertheless, it takes the United States Treasury Department for repairs. My Mercedes was in the repair shop on Friday, December 13. I was driving east on Highway 210 with my mechanic's loaner car on my way to pick up my car. In California, every freeway is always packed. I was driving in lane number 2 (one lane to the right of the fast lane). Suddenly, I had a blowout. Normally, this is no big deal. But on Interstate 210, it's terrifying. I needed to carefully move three lanes to the right to get to the shoulder. My heart was racing, and my hands were shaking. What in the world must I do now? Once I had my wits about me, I was about to call AAA to rescue me. As I was ready to dial the number, a big California highway emergency service truck pulled up behind me. The driver said, "I'm here to help you." The fact that he stopped so quickly was totally amazing. You have no idea how scary it is to get out of your car and watch and listen to the traffic going by at a relatively high speed. The nice man pulled out his equipment, changed my tire, and was about to return to his truck.

I said to him, "How much do I owe you?"

He replied, "Nothing."

I said, "You gotta be kidding me!"

He said, "No, your California taxes have already taken care of the bill."

The point I'm making here is that I believe with all my heart that this man was an angel. I share this story because, throughout my seventy-three years on this earth, it's without a doubt that I have had many angels protecting me. As you read this book, it will be clear to you that I have had a multitude of angels watching over me.

The best angel in my life is one I'm completely aware of, my dear and beautiful wife, Nancy. Nancy, as a nurse, wanted to know my medical risk factors. She knew that my birth mother, Evelyn, died prematurely at age forty-eight. She was uncertain of my mother's risk factors. Both Nancy and I were uncertain about who my biological father was. Nancy started looking at old photographs and asking questions about my past to many of my extended family. Intriguing! Over the past years, we received information from reliable family members about my birth father. This quest for information has lead me to write this book.

After sharing my story with Rev. Jim Kok, he insisted, on several occasions, that I write this story of my life. Being a good codependent with a high need to please, I obeyed.

The picture on the front cover of this is me as a kid. His name is Little Ricky. He's a cute, little guy, don't you agree? A long time ago, I read a poem that said, "There will only be kindergartners in Heaven." It's an interesting concept that very few people think about. However, Jesus said, "Unless you become like a little child, you cannot enter the kingdom of God" (Mark 10:13–15 NIV). Furthermore, as I grew older, Little Ricky grew further and further away from my mind and my consciousness. It wasn't until I entered my therapy program that I was reminded to remember, reclaim, and treat that child within me with care and kindness. More of this concept will be revealed as you read my story. Finally, when I was conceived and born, God knew that I would need many angels protecting me throughout my whole life. So, this Little Ricky is in the center of the *Circle of Trust*.

Many of you probably have seen the very funny and touching movie *Meet the Parents*. There is one part of the movie where the father (played by Robert De Niro) of the future bride talks to his future son-in-law played by Ben Stiller. He says, "Good morning, Greg. Last night, you learned a little secret about the Burns family. If you keep your mouth shut for the rest of your life, you are in no immediate danger. With the knowledge that you've been given, you are now inside of what I like to call the Burns' circle of trust. I keep nothing from you, and you keep nothing from me ... and 'round and 'round we go. Alright?"

I also have a circle of trust. This circle of trust is God the Father, God the Son, Jesus Christ, and God the Holy Spirit. This book is the story of my life. The book will be short, sweet, bittersweet, intriguing, and amazing. My story is complicated, but if you pay attention, it will be a good read.

I'm an ordained minister in the Christian Reformed Church. For most of my career, I served as a chaplain in psychiatric hospitals. In my work as a pastoral counselor, obtaining a personal genogram is essential. A genogram is a family tree on paper. It always helps me to better understand a person's history and their support system. Therefore, I'm now including my own genogram for your understanding. I hope this will give you a clear picture of my family and my origins. It will also give you a reference to look back as you read my story.

Evelyn's Family Tree:
Eric's Mother

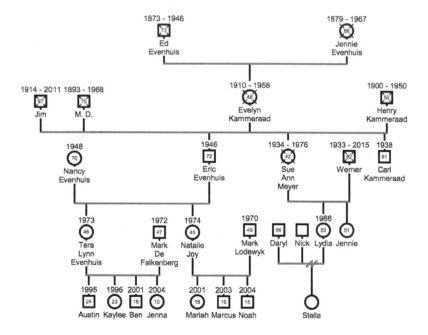

One

❦

My Early Years (Birth to Twelve)

My origin begins with Grandma Jennie Evenhuis, who was an incredible woman. She had three siblings (I've included a picture of her two brothers, Robert and Simon, and her sister Anna, refer to Picture XX). Jennie is the young woman on the right with the big hat. She was so stunningly beautiful; it only led me to believe that my grandpa Ed Evenhuis was a very fortunate man to have married such a smart and beautiful woman. Jennie's maiden name was Poole. All of her siblings, and their children, were very intelligent and prominent citizens of western Michigan. My grandpa Ed died in 1946; the same year I was born. I never met him. Grandma Evenhuis lived to be eighty-eight years old.

As you can see from her latest picture, she never lost her style and class. I have many fond memories being with my grandma Evenhuis. One outstanding memory I have is that every birthday I received a card in the mail with a one-dollar bill. Those cards are such treasured memories of mine.

Ed and Jennie had six children. I also have a photograph of all the Evenhuis children (see picture XX). From top left to right are Seymor, Martha, and Richard, Evelyn (my mother), and Robert (my uncle who adopted me). Front and center is John, the eldest, who died of the Spanish flu epidemic in 1920 at only twenty years old. It's important to note that John's death had a profound effect on the entire Evenhuis family. John was larger than life, both physically and in his outgoing personality. Throughout the history of the Evenhuis family, John's memory was kept alive through stories of his faith in Jesus Christ and John's kind heart.

Now that you have a better understanding of my family background, I can now inform you of my nativity. I was born on Monday, July 29, 1946, in Zeeland, Michigan. My mother absolutely adored me. I was a chubby, cuddly, little baby boy. I was the youngest of three children: Sue Ann, Carl, and me. My sister was twelve years older than me, and my brother was eight years older. Due to these age differences, we had different experiences, and we were never close as siblings. In addition, I was also the youngest of all my Evenhuis cousins.

As you can see from my genogram in the introduction, my mother's name was Evelyn Kammeraad. She was married to Henry Kammeraad. This is where my story gets very interesting. In order to research my medical history, I discovered many fascinating facts about my family. According to a popular family history website, my mother was previously married to a man in St. Joseph, Michigan. In asking questions of my family members, I learned that my mother had thought her first husband was a medical student. And when this turned out to be false, she divorced him. Somewhere in her journey, she met Henry Kammeraad. A painter, Henry was eight years older than my mother. And I learned that he also was previously married without children. Henry and Evelyn were married on September 9, 1933. Henry was thirty-three, and my mother was twenty-five years old. Sue Ann was born in 1934. Carl was born in 1938.

We know for sure that Henry was one of six children to Frank and Jacoba Kammeraad. We also know that all his siblings were respectable people. Oral tradition has it that Henry was the black sheep of the family. He contracted work as a painter for high-risk jobs, such as church steeples and water towers. He also painted elaborate high-end homes in East Grand Rapids. In addition, we know that he liked to drink, gamble, and hated Michigan winters. He left the family for the warm breezes of Florida during the cold, dreary Michigan winters. My brother Carl informed me that Henry and Evelyn had separated during the last four years of Henry's life. He also said that our mother had a great respect for Henry's father, Frank. I learned Frank was also called Franz. I was probably named after him. My full name is Eric Franz. This made me feel very happy that my mother named me after a well-respected and hardworking man. Because Henry was the black sheep, I conjectured that his father tried to set him up in the business, for Frank was a painter and decorator too. But I don't think it worked out well.

I did find Henry Kammeraad's obituary in the *Grand Rapids Press*. He died in 1950, but the cause of death was unknown. At the time of this research, I assumed that Henry Kammeraad was my father, since his name was on my birth certificate. I never looked like my father, Henry; nor did I look my brother and sister, Carl and Sue Ann; and finally, I never had the same temperament as these people. It's always an interest to me that I had an intuitive hunch that my real birth father was a medical doctor.

The obituary stated that Evelyn was his surviving wife, though Carl thought they were divorced. After an abusive incident in 1945, I surmise that Henry and Evelyn were separated from 1945 to 1950, the time of his death. The fact that I never knew Henry is probably because he and my mother were separated. In fact, I don't even remember his death, as I was only four years old.

This is where my life story gets even more curious. I was conceived at the end of October 1945. I like to think that it was on Reformation Day. I was a true Calvinist right from the very start. When my mother found out she was pregnant, she wanted to abort me. I learned this from one of our visits with my aunt Martha, Evelyn's older sister. Aunt Martha was the truth-teller in the family. She also told me that there was a Christian medical doctor who also convinced my mother to do the right thing. In addition, my cousin Jim Evenhuis informed me that he learned from his mother, Mable, that abortion was an option. Aunt Mable, Jim's mother, was also my mother's best friend. To this day, I believe Martha, Mable, and the good doctor urged my mother to keep me. At that time, abortions were illegal. Being in the medical profession, my mother had the ways and means to accomplish an illegal abortion. Obviously, she heeded everyone's wise counsel and advice. Because I was spared, you can understand why I'm pro-life all the way.

For Nancy and me, our detective work continued, as my story gets *even more* interesting. In June 2016, I visited my cousin Jim Evenhuis. He shared that he was undergoing treatment for kidney cancer. It became more urgent for me to visit him. Prior to my visit, I had asked him to inform me of any information about who he thought was my father. I suspected that he knew because he was ten years older than me and he was Mable's son.

After a wonderful visit, and just before I left, I said, "Jim, who's my father?'"

And without any hesitation, he said it was Dr. ——.

I said, "Wow! This is all starting to make sense!" Keeping in mind that the good doctor could be my father was a startling possibility. I find it interesting that intuitively I often joked and speculated that my father was a surgeon.

So now we started our research regarding information about the good doctor. Suffice to say, he was a very fine man. Nancy and I knew that my mother knew this man well. She was his office nurse. Carl also informed us that we lived in the house adjacent to his office in my early years. Also in our research, I found photographs of the good doctor. The resemblances between the two of us are remarkable. In further research, we learned that the good doctor delivered me, according to my birth certificate. The ultimate convincing evidence was when I learned from the family tree website that I have second and third cousins with the good doctor's name. Finally, my mother would often take me to his office for routine physicals and checkups. I do remember these visits well. I can only surmise that Mom wanted to reassure him that I was a healthy child. I do remember him being a very kind man.

You may ask, "How does this make Eric feel?"

Both my sister and brother were challenges to my mother and to me. My sister Sue was overbearing and problematic to me. I have very few memories of her. She did graduate from the University of Michigan. She became a public health nurse. Unfortunately, she was killed in a car accident in the San Francisco, California, area in July 1976.

It is a known fact that Henry Kammeraad drank too much alcohol. He abandoned the family during the winter months by running off to Florida. We know that he gambled on the horses, and he was abusive to my mother. The fact that he was abusive was scandalous to the Dutch community in that era. Because of this irresponsible behavior, I was relieved to learn that I'm not his son. My mother separated from Henry for the remainder of his life. I was also elated that my intuition about my father being a doctor turned out to be true! I think my mother truly loved and respected the doctor and that he also loved and respected my mother. Due to confidentiality, I can say nothing more about the good doctor, even though I know who he is. I found it remarkable that my mother was able to preserve his reputation and she didn't disclose any truth about my origin.

Now I want to talk about another part of my life: Jim Schilstra. Jim was a master sergeant, medic, and chaplain's assistant in the United States Army. He served honorably in the Korean War. My mother was a nurse who cared for both of his parents in the Zeeland Hospital. In 1942, Jim was called home to be at their bedside at the time of their impending death. While visiting his parents, Jim began a romantic relationship with my mother.

In addition to being an honorable soldier, he was an honorable man. Jim told us that since my mother was married to Henry, he wouldn't interfere. Since he didn't need his monthly pay while in the service, he sent that money to my mother to provide her with financial support. After Henry Kammeraad's death, Jim married my mother. I remember the wedding, and I remember the reception at the Pantland Hotel in Grand Rapids. I remember the chef slicing a baron of beef. People couldn't believe how much I ate. It was a fun evening. After Nancy and I were married, we speculated that perhaps Jim was my father. We had a very frank talk with Jim about the possibility that he could be my father. We believed that he spoke the truth to us. After mom died, Nancy and I continued to keep in touch with Jim. Jim lived in Granville, Michigan, a suburb of Grand Rapids. Nancy and I would often meet with him for dinner when I was a student at Calvin College. On one particular evening, we flat out asked him if he could have been my father. He categorically denied it with tears in his eyes. After Jim and my mother were married, a new life began for me.

We moved to 741 Oakdale Street in Grand Rapids. My sister was in Ann Arbor at the University of Michigan, where she was getting her master's degree in public health nursing. I remember moving to Grand Rapids. Carl was living with us in the bedroom next to me. Carl was an interesting brother. First of all, he was extremely intelligent. I remember that he built his own radio from scratch. He wrapped copper wire around a small cardboard tube with other gizmos. I remember that when he turned it on, it worked! In addition to being intelligent, once he had a brush with the law. As an adolescent, Carl had many problems. One day when I was very young—five years old—two police officers came to our door in Grand Rapids. They asked to see "Ricky Kammeraad." With my mother's wonderful sense of humor, she brought me to the door and said, "Here he is." My only conclusion is that when Carl got into trouble, he used my name instead of his own. I'm not sure if Carl ever graduated from high school, but when he was eighteen years old, he joined the army. However, it wasn't long before he was granted a medical discharge. It's also very interesting to know that the same doctor also signed his medical discharge with full disability. Since then, he has been well taken care of by our wonderful government. He now lives independently in California. I'm his next-of-kin emergency contact, and I'm glad that we have reconnected. He's eighty-one years old, and I'm so proud of him. It was just recently that I reconnected with Carl. He is presently living independently in Menlo Park, California. My cousin Marie Slate was regularly in touch with Carl, looking after his best welfare. Since her death, Nancy and I have now taken the place of Marie's caregiving.

I'm so happy that I now have an opportunity to visit with Carl periodically. I'm also extremely proud that he is doing so well. He has been a valuable source of information regarding my family of origin. His memory at eighty-one years old is very sharp. He has proved to be a good resource for this book.

Nancy once asked him, "What do you remember about Eric as a younger brother?"

He replied, "He was always an encouragement to me." I was shocked and pleased! When I was in second grade at seven years of age, Jim was hired as a postal worker in Grandville, Michigan. We moved to Grandville to be closer to Jim's work and also to give Carl a fresh start. It worked out well for Jim, but not for Carl. He was expelled from Grandville High School; he then joined the army.

Life in Grandville was a dream for me. I loved school. Mom and Jim bought me a purebred collie named King. They gave me five-dollar-a-week allowance. I worked for the *Grand Rapids Herald* delivering morning papers. They bought me a new Schwinn bike. I never had an alarm clock. I never had to be told to get up. I woke up on my own; went to my school on my own. I got good grades. I played sports, and I thought I was Bobby Lane, an outstanding, talented quarterback for the Detroit Lions. Bobby Lane's jersey number was 22. At a very young age, he became my role model, idol, and inspiration to play football. I played quarterback for the school. I played Little League baseball as a sidearm pitcher. I almost pitched a no-hitter one time. Top of the sixth inning, a batter had a base hit to the right-center field with a stand-up triple. I'll never forget it. The coach and the team gave me a lot of praise. It was a great memory.

Unfortunately, there were dark clouds forming. Mom was working at Blodgett Hospital as a nurse and drinking quite heavily. Unbeknownst to me, she was probably using barbiturates as well. She may have been sneaking drugs from the workplace. Because of this, I hated bringing any of my friends home. I never knew what to expect. Did I have a happy, sober mother? Or an intoxicated mother who was passed out on the couch? Nobody did anything to address this problem. In addition to the many things that Jim and my mother provided for me, they bought me a set of the encyclopedia, an erector set, and an electric football game. If Mom was drunk, I would go into my room and read the encyclopedia (I read all the books), or I played with my erector set. I built a fabulous four-foot-high elevator with an electric motor. I could watch the elevator go up or down. I was skilled at entertaining myself.

Another very positive memory was canning tomatoes and peaches with Grandma Jennie Evenhuis. I was the tomato squeezer with my hands, and I was the peach peeler with the paring knife after they were scalded with boiling water. I remember filling mason jars with tomatoes, peaches, and the sugar syrup. I remember putting the jars in a big canning pan and waiting for the lids to pop. That pop was a sign that the process was successful.

LIGHTNING STRIKES

On September 14, 1958, thunder and lightning struck. Early Sunday morning, Jim summoned me to help him lift my dead mother onto the bed. She was cold, blue, and very heavy. Jim lifted from her shoulders, and I lifted her legs. It was the most awful moment of my life. This was a very shocking event for a twelve-year-old kid. I think Jim knew she was dead. After all, he was a medic in the army. This wasn't the first time he'd seen a dead body. He told me to go deliver my Sunday morning papers, which I did. When I came back, Mom's body was gone.

Jim said they took her to the hospital. I spent the rest of the day with my friend John Heyboer. I kind of knew that she was dead, but never received the definitive word that she had passed. I remember sitting on the back steps of John's house in Grand Rapids, Michigan. Jim and my uncle Rich, my mom's brother, got out of the car and walked to the back steps. I knew right away from the look on their faces that Mom was dead. And indeed, they told me that this was the truth.

I sobbed and sobbed and sobbed. They all were very comforting to me, especially Jim. I don't remember, but I think he cried too. Mom was only forty-eight years old, way too young to die. At the time, I never asked what the cause of death was. That Saturday night, she had been finishing up the canning of the tomatoes, and she left a note that said, "Ricky, take the tomatoes down to the cellar." I later learned the death certificate said pulmonary edema.

Mom's funeral was scheduled for Wednesday, September 17. Jim asked me if I wanted to go to the viewing at the funeral home. I said no. One evening after a visitation, Don and Dorothy Walters came to the house. The Walter's visit was a very significant part of my life that I will explain later. They owned a farm in Overisel, Michigan. My mother made arrangements for me to spend part of the summers on the farm. I remember that Dorothy Walters was the first person to hug me, and she said the weirdest thing, something you should never say at a funeral to a grieving kid. "If you ever want to live with us, call me." I will never forget that! She must have known something that I didn't. The first time I saw my mother in the casket was on the day of the funeral. I was the last to be escorted into the room. I was led down the aisle with Jim and Carl on each side of me. Carl looked very sharp in his army uniform. I was happy to have both of them for support. As I approached the casket, I couldn't believe what I saw. My mother was dressed in a beautiful gray dress, with a beautiful silver necklace. I don't remember this, but people told tell me I had picked a small bouquet of flowers from the yard and placed them in the casket. I don't remember the funeral director closing the casket. I guess I just wasn't looking. I must have had my head down. I do remember the minister's sermon though and the verse he used. "For my thoughts are not your thoughts, neither are your ways my ways, declares the Lord. As the Heavens are higher than the Earth, so are my ways higher than your ways and my thoughts than your thoughts" (Isaiah 55:8 NIV). The word of God is still the best comfort in grief. The next thing I remember about the funeral was riding in the limousine to the cemetery. I was fascinated with the power windows. The entire way to the cemetery, I was pushing the windows up and down. I can only imagine that I was driving people nuts, but nobody said anything about it. More kindness for little Ricky.

Just recently, I read the guest list of all the people who came to Mom's funeral. What impressed me the most was that my third-, fourth-, and fifth-grade teachers attended this service. They were Mrs. Marshall (who taught me to read), Mrs. Kunzi (who taught me about rules and discipline), and Miss Breems (she was a beautiful woman—I had a huge crush on her). In addition, I was amazed how many people attended my mom's funeral. It was obvious that my mother was a very well-loved and respected person. The next day, which was a Thursday, everything went back to normal again. I wish I had a grief therapist, but perhaps in those days nobody knew anything about grief therapy.

Now if you think this drama was over, forget about it. It continued to get worse. After Mom died, Jim and I lived together in Grandville. I would go to school, and then we would have dinner with Jim's sister Gert and Harvey Coombs every night. Harvey and Gert had two kids, Riley and Marylynn. Riley and I were approximately the same age, and we became grand friends. In the meantime, Jim Schilstra met Alta. Alta was just getting out of a divorce, and Jim was a new widower. Alta saw the opportunity to marry a man who would take care of her for the rest of her life. Jim married Alta in June of 1959. This was nine months after my mother died. The reason I'm including this story is because Alta was the catalyst for a major life-changing event. Approximately fifteen years ago, Jim wrote me a lengthy letter about different events in his life. In that letter, he wrote about Alta, "Looking back, I think I was too hasty to remarry. If I was Catholic, I [would] have annulled this marriage."

At the time Jim was married to Alta, my brother Carl came home on leave from the army, and my sister Sue came home from college. Even though this situation was temporary, Jim wrote, "With them all being home, Alta must have figured it was more than she desired." Alta told Jim she was thinking of getting an apartment.

On a hot summer day, August 10, 1959, Alta took Jim's car, all of her belongings, and moved out. This was a complete and total surprise to me. Nothing that I could perceive precipitated her leaving. When I came home that day, everything that Alta owned was gone. I didn't say this at the time, but I know I thought, *This is ridiculous!* I remembered, vividly, the words of Dorothy Walters: "If you ever want to live with us, just call." I called Dorothy and told her I was ready for her to pick me up. I packed my little suitcase, and she was there within the hour. She brought me back to her home in Overisel, Michigan. I felt like this was home. Obviously, Dorothy called Jim to tell him what had happened and where I was. Jim drove to the farm, and pleaded with me to come back. I think it was only God's strength that allowed me to tell Jim there was no way I was ever coming back.

FOSTER HOME

Our detective work continued. Don and Dorothy Walters were foster parents. They had a small sixty-acre farm in Overisel, a small settlement of Dutch farmers. Ever since I was little, I had spent many memorable and happy summers with the Walters. I always wondered how my mother, Evelyn, made connections with these people. It's no longer a mystery to me. Two years ago, Nancy and I met with Shirley, Dorothy Walters's sister. Obviously, she is older now. Nevertheless, she revealed more truth. She was a social worker for Ottawa County who arranged for Carl and me to be placed under their care as foster children. I was around three years old, and Carl was around eleven. She never told me why we were placed in their home. I speculate that mom may have had financial challenges raising her three children. Social services may have been contacted because of Henry's irresponsible and abusive behavior. Perhaps my brother Carl spent more time with the Walters than I did. I only remember being there in the summertime. I never missed any school. It was a very wonderful experience for me.

When I first met the Walters, they had no children. Soon, they adopted a baby named David. This adoption may have been arranged through Shirley. Shortly after the adoption, Dorothy miraculously became pregnant with Donna, then Duane, and Diane—all in short succession. Part of my happiness with this family was playing with these four children.

Another part of the joy was being an active participant in farm life. I helped with the cows, pigs, chickens, even the harvest. It was a big deal to drive the tractor in the field while the farmers would load the trailer with sheaves of wheat. After the trailer was loaded, I would drive the loaded trailer to the thrashing machine. Harvesting was a community event. The local farmers would help each other with the harvest. They would lease a thrashing machine that was then passed on to the neighboring farmer. I remember the air was filled with excitement, energy, and friendship. There was always a prayer and scripture reading after the noon lunch.

One day, one of the farmers said to the host, "Make it short, because we have a lot of work to do!" Then the host proceeded to read the longest psalm in the Bible, Psalm 119. Never tell a stubborn Dutchman what to do!

POWER IN MOTION

My decision to leave Jim set many wheels in motion for events that would happen to little Ricky. I stayed with Don and Dorothy Walters for five months. I went to school at Sandy View Elementary School in Overisel. I loved it there. It was during this time that I went to a Youth for Christ rally in Grand Rapids, Michigan. Harvey Coombs arranged for me to attend the rally. I don't remember what the speaker spoke of, other than an invitation to come forward to give your heart and life to Jesus Christ. I wanted to go forward, and my heart was soft, and the Holy Spirit was nudging me; I didn't want to miss the bus.

The speaker said, "If you come forward, the buses will wait for you." That gave me permission to come forward. That was the night that I turned my life over to Jesus Christ. During my growing up, my mother never really brought me to church. I went periodically to a Baptist Sunday school, but only because the Sunday school bus would pick me up in front of my house in Grandville. When I was with Don and Dorothy Walters, they had a Marian's Children's Bible storybook. I was an avid reader, and I read the entire book in one sitting.

After reading the book, I asked Dorothy Walters, "Why did they kill a nice man like Jesus?" I'm sure she gave me a good answer, but I don't remember it. I only know that it was the Holy Spirit beginning His work in my life. The story of Jesus touched me. It's true that the heart of a child is soft, particularly a grieving child who lost his mother. When my mother died, the Grandville newspaper called and asked me, "What church did your mother attend?" I said I think it was the Methodist church. I didn't know what to say, so I said what came to my mind, and they put it in the paper. It does give me pause to understand why my mother, who was raised in a good Christian Reformed Church, basically left the church. Something went awry somewhere. The wheels that were turning were fueled by Grandma Jennie Evenhuis. In addition, my sister Sue, Jim Schilstra, and my uncle Robert and my aunt Faye Evenhuis. Reverend Robert and Faye Evenhuis were the host and hostess of the Manor House at Knollcrest Campus, where the new Calvin College was to be built. The Manor House was a mansion, the most beautiful house I've ever been in. The college rebuilt two bathrooms in rich granite. I've never been in a more beautiful bathroom in my life. My uncle Robert was hired to host wealthy people and dignitaries who would give generous donations for the development of the Knollcrest Campus.

On one particular Thanksgiving Day, all the family were invited to the Manor House for dinner. I was sitting next to Uncle Robert when he leaned over and asked me, "Is there anything you would like, Ricky?"

I said, "Yes, I would like a 7-Up."

Shortly thereafter, the maid came to Robert's side. He said, "Ricky would like a glass of 7-Up." Out of nowhere, the maid, Addie, came out with a silver tray, a glass of ice, and a can of 7-Up. I thought, *How did this happen?* I felt like I was royalty at the House of Windsor.

Later, I learned that Uncle Robert had a little button at his foot that would buzz the maid. It was amazing!

In January of 1960, Jim came to talk to me and asked if I would like to go to Pease, Minnesota, to live with Uncle Robert and Aunt Faye. Uncle Robert had just accepted a call from the Pease Christian Reformed Church and would be moving there in February. Michigan winters are really depressing—no sunshine for many days, with cold temperatures. I knew nothing about Minnesota winters. Nevertheless, it was the promise of a new beginning for me. I told Jim that I thought I'd accept this offer. I packed up my suitcase again. Jim and I traveled to the Manor House, where the four of us had a ham-and-baked-potato dinner. This was the last time that I'd see Jim for a long time. It felt sad to say goodbye to Jim, but it was also an anticipation of leaving Michigan for a new life in Minnesota, which I knew nothing about. As I reflect back, I think I was ready to leave Michigan, and away from all the misery, grief, and heartache. So the next day we traveled to Holland, Michigan, and picked up Faye's mother, Effie. We traveled to Minnesota. Halfway to Minnesota, we stopped at a motel and spent the night. The next morning, we had breakfast. Aunt Faye said to me, "Ricky, you can have anything you want for breakfast." I thought, *This is wonderful!* The waitress came and asked for my order, and I said, "I'd like toast and tomatoes." This was my favorite breakfast. Immediately, Aunt Faye said, "You can't have that!" I knew I was in trouble. This was the beginning of my new learning curve with Faye.

I must tell you that I knew absolutely nothing about Pease, Minnesota. It was a small village. Only 191 people lived in this town. But the church was huge. Pease was a farming community of many Dutch people. As we were driving into Pease, Aunt Faye said, "Ricky, we'll just pretend that you have always been our son."

At the time, I thought, *This is just fine. I won't have to share with anyone anything about my painful past.* And so life began anew.

This is where it all began, my
grandmother Jennie Evenhuis

This is the family photo of Grandma Jennie with her
sister and two brothers, Anna, Robert, and Simon Poole

My grandmother, a beautiful, young
woman with style and class

These are the Evenhuis children born to Jennie
and Ed Evenhuis. The top row from left to right is
Seymore, Martha, and Richard. The bottom row is
Evelyn, my mother; John, and Robert, my uncle.

Martha (on the right) and Evelyn

Evelyn Evenhuis in her nursing uniform at graduation

Evelyn with Sue, Carl and Ricky

My sister Sue at her nursing graduation
from University of Michigan

My brother Carl and me

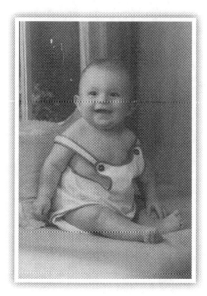

My baby picture

I don't know if I trust this bearded man

Go get 'em coyboy

My favorite companion, King, a pure breed collie

I hit it out of the park

My fifth grade school picture, the year my mother died

My mother Evelyn and my step dad, Jim Schilstra

My mother Evelyn's last professional
photograph before her death

Aerial view of the farm

My earliest memory of the farm with Don Walters

Not sure I should drive this tractor

Don and his adopted son, David and me

Dorothy, David and me

David, Duane and Donna Walters and me (after I
ran away to their farm and stayed with them from
September to February) photo taken December 7,1959
and in February 1960 I moved to Pease, Minnesota

Two

❧❧❧

My Minnesota Years (Twelve to Eighteen)

T hank God that chapter 1 is over. My childhood life was complicated, and filled with joy and tragedy. My Minnesota years were an adjustment filled with discipline and a very strong sense of family. After the toast-and-tomato fiasco, we drove off Highway 169 into the small, little village of Pease, Minnesota. I noticed that the highway sign said Population 191. That number stays in my memory. It was a very cold February day. It was colder than any day I'd ever experienced in Michigan. As I mentioned, coming to Pease was a new beginning, a fresh start, and a new chapter in my life. As we pulled into the driveway of the church, I saw the parsonage. This was the biggest house I have ever lived in. The parsonage was a large, two-story, four-bedroom home. I felt amazed. Of course, the house was vacant. As I explored the first floor, I couldn't believe how big the kitchen, dining room, living room, and downstairs bedroom were. As I walked upstairs, there was a huge bathroom, a large study for Dad, three really big bedrooms, and a large landing at the top of the stairs. I chose the bedroom that was closest to the bathroom.

After we moved in, Aunt Faye removed all of the wallpaper and repainted all the rooms. They bought me a huge braided, oval rug that perfectly matched the paint on the walls. I also remember a brand-new, queen-size bed with wooden frame. When I settled in, and as the furniture arrived, I felt excited, elevated, and respected. What was happening to my simple life that I left behind in Michigan? Many people from the church came to the house to welcome us. They came bearing gifts, food, flowers, and much more. I had never, ever been treated like this in my whole life.

My father was given a new name—I had no idea what it meant. It was Dominie. I later learned that this was a common name given to the pastor of a Dutch church. The actual meaning of Dominie is *Lord*. Now Uncle Robert became "Dad," and Aunt Faye became "Mom," as Aunt Faye told me to just call them that. Having a mom and dad felt really good. I suddenly had a new home with many people who cared about me. Many events were quickly set in motion. The first Friday night, prior to Dad's first Sunday as their pastor, we had an official church welcome. Dad was all dressed up in his best. Mom looked absolutely beautiful, carrying in her arms two dozen red roses. For the first time in my life, I was dressed in a suit, tie, and a starched white shirt. The program included many welcoming speeches. Then we were greeted by every member of the congregation. A line formed to greet us. They shook my hand warmly. I didn't even know these people welcoming me to this amazing community. I remember that night, lying in my bed, thinking, *This is unreal. I didn't know that a life like this ever existed.*

That following Sunday, Dad was officially installed as the pastor of the Pease Christian Reformed Church. Church service started at 10:00 a.m. I was thinking that we'd need to go to church early, as there were so many people, but I was told we didn't need to go until two minutes before church. As we entered the church doors, I saw that every seat was full. We were ushered into the best seat in the building. After I sat down, I saw a small bronze plaque that said Reserved. I'd never, ever had a seat reserved for me in my whole life. I felt special, and I must say that this special feeling never went away my whole life. Shortly after we sat down, Dad came up the stairs from the church basement, followed by ten elders. Dad took his seat on the pulpit. The elders all sat in a row reserved for the elders. What was funny about that was they seemed to pop up like gophers coming out of the ground. To be honest, I wanted to laugh, but I knew instinctively that this was a serious moment. I became aware that this was a formal and sacred service.

Since it was winter (February), the next thing I learned was that there was another church service at 2:00 p.m., a repeat performance, but a different sermon. My first thought was, *Do we have to do this again?* Indeed, we did. Having never gone to church before, this was a shocker. There was no more pro football on Sunday afternoon, no more Walt Disney on TV. There was nothing on Sunday but church. Suddenly, the special feeling seemed to lose its charm! So after the second service was over, I went to church for the third time for young people's society. I said, "This is too much!" To add more shock to my system, I quickly learned that on Wednesday night, there was catechism. Dad also taught this class. Catechism is a summary of the Christian faith. In addition, I needed to memorize the long answers to the catechism questions. As shocking as my former days were, I did have a deep sense of family. My heart had longed for belonging.

The first pastoral crisis that I experienced was the death of Wendal Vedders. Wendal was a high school senior who died when he was overcome by fumes in the silo. His family called Dad early in the morning. And Dad called us, Mom and I, to come to the kitchen table for prayer. He prayed, Mom prayed, and I was expected to pray. I didn't know how to pray, so I said, "God, be with this family that wasn't so lucky today." Afterward, Dad said, "Son, we don't believe in luck. You may want to say they weren't so fortunate." Dad was gentle and kind; it was a great teaching moment for me. I have never forgotten it. Ever since that moment, whenever I hear the word *luck*, I want to make a correction by saying we don't believe in luck.

The funeral for Wendel was packed. Dad had an amazing, comforting sermon. I will never forget the hymn they sang, "When Peace like a River." This was the first death that I'd experienced since my mother's passing, which had been about two years previous. I think Wendel's death was significant because of the comfort that it gave me regarding my own mother's death.

Surprisingly, I became very attentive to Dad's sermons. I thought he was a great preacher, and he explained a biblical text extremely well. I was amazed how there was so much to be taught from just one biblical story. I found it to be very interesting and informative. Dad's preaching made the Word of God come alive for me. He always explained the Word of God, and he also applied it in a practical way to our lives. For example, one Sunday night he preached about the man who was possessed by demons. "After being healed, the demon possessed man begged to go with Jesus. But Jesus said, 'No, go home and tell your family how much the Lord has done for you'" (Mark 5:1–21 NIV). That night was a turning point in my relationship with Dad. It was summer. A thunderstorm was brewing in the northwestern skies of Minnesota. It was very still, and warm. Dad and I were sitting on the back porch, watching the thunderclouds roll in as Dad smoked his pipe. In the distance, we saw lightning and heard great booms of thunder. The smoke from Dad's pipe lazily drifted upward. I told Dad what wonderful things Jesus had done for me in my life and how much I loved Jesus. He was listening, and he accepted me. He was quiet. I knew that we made a real bond and an attachment that night. As I look back now, I see more than ever what a profound, positive effect Dad had on my life. I will share more later. I want to note that I did write a book about my father's prayers. Dad could preach, pray, and bring me to the very presence of God.

AUNT FAYE

Well, those were the some of the many highs that I experienced in Pease. There were also the lows. Regretfully, I have to say that all of the lows were centered around Aunt Faye. I struggle with what I should say about Faye. First of all, I know without a doubt that she did love me. I loved her too. After all, she did make a positive and loving decision to take me in after the death of my mother. Faye was also much more assertive than Dad. So I came to the conclusion that their decision to take me in was no doubt strongly supported by Faye.

Having said that, Faye was also a very difficult person in my formative years. Without being specific, there were times when Faye was abusive, controlling, demanding, and invasive. I must also say that Faye was the perfect minister's wife. She always wanted Dad and me to look good. She had exquisite taste in clothing. As a minister's wife, she made every effort to invite every family member from the church to the parsonage where she would prepare a fine meal. I became her sous chef, and she taught me many wonderful things about baking and food preparation.

She also taught me how to be a gracious host, with warm hospitality. She definitely had a spiritual gift of hospitality. I take with me these gifts of hospitality to this very day, and I still enjoy reaching out and inviting people to our home. When people from the church came to our home, I totally enjoyed listening to stimulating conversations around the dining room table. I thank Faye for initiating and providing these wonderful events.

There were also things that shocked me. Shocker number one was when the three of us were sitting in the living room after Dad preached on Sunday morning. Aunt Faye literally ripped into Dad's sermon. I couldn't believe the intense criticism and anger that came forth. At the time, I wasn't necessarily protective of Dad. First of all, I thought just getting up and preaching in front of so many people was a triumph in and of itself. I never thought Dad ever had a bad sermon. To hear Aunt Faye's critical spirit was dumbfounding to me. After Dad died, I read many of his typewritten sermons. At the end of many sermons, he would personally write, "Mom didn't like this sermon," and then he would add a prayer: "Lord, make me a worthy servant." To be honest, it broke my heart. He must have bought her criticism hook, line, and sinker. I'm here to tell you today that her criticism was unnecessary and cruel. That criticism came out of her own mental imbalance and false sense of pride. Dad was humble and grateful to be of use to God, but these criticisms must have eroded his confidence. Nobody in Pease ever saw this side of Faye.

The next low is the acorn story. One warm spring day, Aunt Faye took me out to rake the acorns. The parsonage was on a two-acre lot of land. There were multiple, giant oak trees. The oak trees would drop their acorns in the fall of the year. The winter snow would pack the acorns into the ground. The spring thaw packed them deeper into the ground. Faye took this amazing rake, and with all of her might, she raked a one square yard of grass and acorns. As I was watching her rake, it was unbelievable how many acorns came out of the ground. After a million acorns were released from the ground, she handed me the rake and said, "I want this whole yard to look just like this." Luckily, she couldn't see the expletives in my mind. I begrudgingly continued to rake to my own liking. Aunt Faye was a perfectionist. My next assignment was weeding the garden. The garden was huge and was on the east end of the property, which bordered the home of Les and Ester Ruis. The garden was ten yards wide by fifty yards long. In the garden were planted beans, peas, carrots, radishes, squash, tomatoes, and much more. As a thirteen-year-old, I never really liked to work; I didn't like to get dirty, and weeding was never my thing. So in between the rows, I laid down newspapers, and then laid down on my side with my left hand holding up my head. I weeded with my right hand. My neighbor Ester came out, saw my valiant efforts to rid the garden of all evil, and she completely cracked up laughing. Hypothetically, this would be material for Garrison Kellor's *A Prairie Home Companion*. Reflecting back on this experience, it's now a cherished story for all our grandchildren.

My next low was the most challenging. I'd just gotten a huge adjustment in my life. Coming to Pease was in and of itself a huge adjustment. As a young man of thirteen years old, I wish someone had told Aunt Faye about the five stages of puberty in boys. As time went on, I started realizing that my body was changing.

There were a number of physical changes. And for a young adolescent boy, they were personal. These bodily changes were embarrassing and private for me. My shoulders were getting broader, and my muscles were developing with great definition. I became noticeably stronger and began a regular workout routine of pushups.

I took great pride in working on a farm and bailing hay. I could pack the bales perfectly on the farmer's hay trailer. As I continued in my development, I experienced wet dreams. According to Dr. Barbara Poncelet, a board-certified physician, these events can occur with, or without, sexual dreams and is completely normal. She states that talking to your son, before these things happen, is helpful so that he know what to expect. She continues. "Let your son know that this is a normal part of puberty, and it will go away in time." In addition, Dr. Poncelet states that involuntary erections are another part of male puberty, and they can occur at any time for absolutely no reason at all. It is important to explain to your son that this may happen, and you have little control over it. It will get better as you get older.

Aunt Faye did none of that. Instead of understanding and kindness, her critical shame-based and Protestant moral ethic, slammed me to the wall. Shame was her best weapon. I remember vividly her telling me that my sexuality was disgusting. Fortunately, I recovered with the help of therapy. The big three sins in the Christian Reformed Church were card playing, dancing, and movies. Aunt Faye helped me write a paper on the evils of attending movies. The argument goes that attending movies contributes to the wealth of Hollywood actors. But the coup d'état was, "Don't get caught in a movie theater when Jesus comes again!" After a regional youth rally, Mom and Dad brought the Michigan speakers to Minneapolis. They were gone about three or four hours. While they were gone, I went to a movie with classmates. The movie was *Town without Pity*. The very first scene was a rape scene. I thought, for sure, Jesus was on His way. On the way home from the movie, the car was packed with kids. I was making out with my girlfriend, while she sat on my lap. It was wonderful. When I got home, I was sure that Mom and Dad were already there. The lights were on, but thankfully, no one was home. I crawled into bed, turned out the lights, and they drove into the driveway. To this day, I don't believe they knew of my wild ways. The next morning, Aunt Faye made me eggs for breakfast. I walked out the door to go to work, and I threw up. My whole being was filled with shame, anxiety, and fear. It was terrible. It was a secret that I kept from them forever.

Another experience I had centered around the church's bell tower speakers. These speakers were very loud, and they were used to call to worship each Sunday morning. This was done by a playing a record, which played chimes. So my friend and I bought the record, *Wipeout,* and if you know the song, it starts with a loud drum solo with the singer crying out, "Wipeout!" On one Friday night church potluck, my friend and I put this record on the church bell tower speaker system. Then we split the scene. Some of the elders rushed to the speaker to remove this record. Mom and Dad never knew I was the culprit.

Another memorable event centered around the sin of dancing. My first love, Anita, invited me to the Sadie Hawkins dance at the high school. I told her my parents would not let me go to a dance. Anita said, "Tell them you are only going to sell tickets at the dance." And so I told Mom and Dad that I would only sell tickets, and they allowed me to go. Well, you can only sell tickets for about a half an hour. The rest of the night, I was dancing with fair Anita. It was a wonderful time.

Only later, did I find out quite dramatically that one of the elders of the church was attending a local monthly civil defense meeting that took place at the high school in a room directly opposite the dance. After the meeting was over, the elder peeked into the dance party and saw me dancing. It was, of course, his moral duty to report this to my parents. I thought I had gotten away with this one too. But one afternoon, coming home from school, Faye, who was completely hysterical, greeted me at the door. She said, "We found out that you were dancing; you will have to be put under church discipline, and Dad may lose his job." It was as if the end of the world was drawing nigh. "Go upstairs and talk to Dad." And so I went upstairs to his study and told him what had happened. His reaction was just the opposite of Faye's. He could not have been more calm, understanding, and reassuring. My conclusion was that dancing wasn't all that bad. I was never busted for card playing. I never wrote an essay on this topic. Today my favorite games are hearts and playing canasta with my wife. In my outlook, the three cardinal sins of the Christian Reformed Church, carry very little weight with me. I'm sure there are much bigger demons in this life. I guess there are highs and lows in every season of living. The Pease season in my life was wonderful. For sure, there were many more highs than lows. As I look back on my first prayer about luck, it definitely was the beginning of my theological quest. Dad was my best tutor and mentor ever. Pease was good. I'm grateful that Robert and Faye chose to adopt me. It altered the course of my life.

GRANDMA EFFIE, FAYE'S MOTHER

For a short time, Faye's mother, Effie, came to live with us. Effie was an amazing woman. While she lived with us, she made braided rugs. It was a laborious process; she made tubes from old wool suits and then braided the tubes into an oval rug. First, she had to cut the suits apart, and then she created the tubes that were all hand sewn. While sewing, she sang in a wavering, shaky voice, "Jesus paid it all. All to Him I owe." Whenever I hear this song, it is a sweet memory and brings a tear to my eye. And I'm so grateful to her wise advice. She said to me, "Ricky, marry your own kind." This wasn't prejudicial. She was basically stating how important it is to marry a Christian woman with a similar background. This advice did help me. Nancy was from a Christian Reformed Church and a rural background. The most important thing was that she also believed in Jesus as her savior.

In addition, there is still one more incredible story of Grandma Effie. The parsonage had two porches on each end of the house. One porch was open air with about seven wooden steps leading to the sidewalk. In her later days, Grandma Effie was in a wheelchair, and it was my job to tip the wheelchair back and descend one step at a time. It was very easy for me; it was all physics, and Grandma Effie trusted me completely. Never once did we have an accident. On one weekend, her sons, Harvey and Jerome, visited Pease with their wives. These men were Faye's brothers. It was a Friday night, and we were all going out for dinner. Harvey and Jerome were bound and determined that they would take their mother down the steps. I told them I was adept at this and had it down to a science. But they prevailed.

Harvey was a big, tall man (six five) and he was at the back of the wheels holding the handles. Jerome, who was shorter and stronger, was at the foot of the wheelchair. As they proceeded down the steps, they quickly lost control of the wheelchair. The wheelchair, along with Grandma Effie, went bouncing down the steps uncontrollably. Effie was crying out, "Kindra, kindra, kindra" (Dutch for "children")!

Jerome quickly got out of the way. Harvey, on the other hand, tried to hang on to stop the wheelchair, but he failed. The wheelchair hit the sidewalk and tipped on its side. Grandma Effie was still in the chair, but now lying on her side, though unhurt. Harvey, on the other hand, hit his chest on the handles and had a serious injury. Jerome was at the bottom trying to stay safely out of the way.

Jerome wasn't hurt, but maybe a bit annoyed with Harvey, and said, "All I could see was the jolly green giant coming at me." After everyone settled down, we went on to dinner. We all assumed that Harvey's discomfort was just a bruise. The next day, he went to the local hospital and discovered that he'd suffered a heart attack.

THE ADOPTION

I did like certain types of work. I liked to mow the churchyard, and the cemetery yard. I liked to help farmers bail hay. I liked working for Mr. Kiel at the hardware store. One warm afternoon, while I was mowing the churchyard, Aunt Faye came to me with a glass of lemonade and chocolate chip cookies. We sat on the church steps taking a break, and she said, "Dad and I would like to adopt you. Would you like for us to adopt you?" This question seemed to come from left field, and I wasn't expecting it. I guess, in the light of so many highs and lows, I told her I would have to think about this offer.

I did think about it, and the next day I gave them my answer. I said, yes, I would like to be adopted.

At the time, I was thirteen years old, and the adoption took place in Milaca, Minnesota. Milaca was a small town five miles north of Pease, Minnesota. It gets a little complicated here, because I'm thinking back on what this event actually meant for me. At the time, I didn't realize there would be lawyers involved. I recently learned that Jim Schilstra, my stepfather, paid for all the legal fees for my adoption. I was unaware of any legal fees. I distinctly remember sitting in the judge's chambers in Milaca, Minnesota. It was unforgettable, and a momentous legal transaction. The judge asked Robert and Faye if they wanted to legally adopt me, and they said yes. The judge then asked me, "Do you, Eric Franz Kammeraad, want to be legally adopted by Robert and Faye Evenhuis?" I said yep. After this, the judge signed the adoption papers, and my last name became Evenhuis, A new birth certificate was even created. It was now legal. I do remember that there was a lot of love in the judge's chambers on that day.

In my never-ending quest for the truth, last year, I went to Ottawa County to obtain my original birth certificate. Of course, I had to prove to the clerk that I was indeed Eric Franz Kammeraad. I needed to produce all the legal papers from the Milaca court proceedings. When I received the original birth certificate, the clerk said, "Don't lose this certificate, because after today, this certificate will be sealed forever. Not even you can retrieve it." On the birth certificate is the name of the doctor who delivered me at 12:15 a.m.!

Now I would like to preach. Saint Paul says we are no longer slaves to sin, but we are adopted into the family of God by the righteousness, and the sacrifice of Christ Jesus. Whereby we are called children of God by adoption. This is now a profound and mysterious truth to me. Nevertheless, I know without a doubt that because of Christ's suffering, death, and resurrection, our redemption is a most sacred, and legal transaction for the complete forgiveness of all our sins.

Even though there have been a number of lows, there are more highs. Mom and Dad gave me discipline, structure, family life, and security. They gave me a foundation for my spiritual life. They also gave me goals. And best of all, Dad introduced me to my beautiful wife, Nancy. Pease was Dad's best experience in ministry. And for me, growing up in a small Midwest farming community was the best community of faith, love, and Midwest values. I wouldn't trade it for anything. It was a part of my life that influenced and shaped me forever. I graduated from eighth grade at Pease Christian School. It was a very small class.

I attended Milaca High School, which was five miles north of Pease. All in all, Milaca High School was a wonderful experience. In my senior year of 1963, John F. Kennedy was assassinated. Everyone remembers where they were when they heard the news. I was in physics class when the announcement came that our president was dead. The gravity of his death affected me deeply. When my mother died, my world was shaken. Now the whole world was shocked by this death. The events that followed his death touched me deeply. This was a death that was an earthquake because of my untreated grief over my mother's death. Once my mother died, I never realized the deep significance of this event in my life. I graduated from Milaca High School, and my future was already decided. I would attend Calvin College in Grand Rapids, Michigan. It was a very good decision.

This is the Pease Christian Reformed
Church. I arrived there February 1960

This is a picture of my adopted father, Rev. Robert
Evenhuis (who is also my maternal uncle)

This is a picture of my adopted mother, Faye Evenhuis

This is Robert and Faye's son, John Evenhuis and his
wife, Gayle who were both always supportive of me

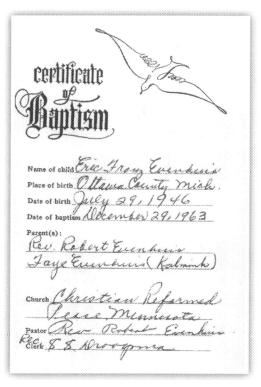

This is my baptism certificate

This is my eighth grade graduation from Pease
Christian School (I'm in the upper left hand corner)

This was my freshman year at Milaca High
School, my homework was overwhelming

My high school graduation picture

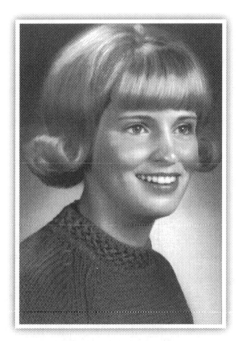

This is my beautiful wife, Nancy Watson, at her high
school graduation from Renville High School

Three

My College and Seminary Years
(Eighteen to Twenty-Eight)

I graduated from Milaca High School in June of 1964. I wish I could remember more about this event. My dad spoke at the baccalaureate service. I also remember having a light-blue robe and spending time with my good friend Don Godeke. Don and I rode to and from school every day. Faye liked Donny because he was, in her eyes, a "goody-goody." I can hear her saying, "Why can't you be more like Donny?" Don was truly a good friend and my best friend in my high school years.

That summer of 1964 was, for me, one of the most significant summers of my life. I met this beautiful girl named Nancy. My father, Robert, visited Nancy's parents when he preached in Renville, Minnesota. Dad was considered a classy man, and thus, the ladies of the church were anxious about hosting him. Since Nancy's mother and father were considered a classy farmer's family, they hosted him. Dad told Nancy and her family many wonderful things about me and my adoption. Nancy says that she was captivated by my story of my adoption. She says that his stories were the beginning of her attraction and compassion for me.

But when Dad came back from Renville, he never mentioned anything about Nancy. Nothing! This summer, I planned to attend the Young Calvinist convention in New Jersey with Robert and Faye. Little did I know, Nancy would also be going to the Young Calvinist convention from her church. Our car caravan met in Baldwin, Wisconsin. It was there I first met Nancy in person for the first time. She was a passenger in the back seat of her pastor's car. I couldn't believe how stunningly beautiful she was. It was love at first sight. As a matter of fact, upon meeting her, I thought, *I think I'm going to marry this woman.*

That is when our love story began. We continued on our journey to New Jersey. At the next stop for gas, Dad and Nancy's pastor, Reverend Van Antwerpen, had a plan. Dad told me I was to kidnap Nancy and drag her into our car. Nancy gave very little resistance. Her pastor had filled her in that this was going to happen. For the rest of the trip to New Jersey, Nancy and I talked and talked. She was a good listener and a good conversationalist. You may say we had an arranged marriage.

The Young Calvinist convention was almost canceled because of the race riots in Patterson, New Jersey. But since it was held in the suburbs of Patterson, they made the decision to proceed with the convention. Throughout the event I took every opportunity to look for Nancy and to be seated together. The last night of the convention was a banquet at a private golf course. The scene couldn't have been more beautiful and romantic. I asked Nancy to be my date. I was wearing a seersucker sport coat, white shirt, and tie. Nancy was stunningly beautiful in a pink, linen sheath dress. Reverend James Lont was the speaker. I don't remember a word he said. I only had eyes for Nancy. Following the banquet, I drove with Nancy, Mom, and Dad to Nancy's host family. Mom and Dad were in the back seat, and we got hopelessly lost. Her directions were useless, and we ended up on Straight Street, which was the heart of the race riots earlier that summer. It was 2:00 a.m., and it was a hot night; many people were outside on their porches drinking beer. I remember vividly, young people with chains banging them on the garbage cans and knocking the garbage cans over. It was a nightmare, and a surreal scene. A carload of white people in a totally African American neighborhood. Faye screamed, "Eric get us out of here!" She voiced what everyone in the car was feeling! Nancy was hugging the passenger door. She was terrified and embarrassed that she didn't know the way home. Looking back, there were a legion of angels surrounding our car. Somehow, we proceeded to get on the New Jersey turnpike headed to New York. I knew it was the wrong way, and there were many emergency turnarounds where I could have made a U-turn. But my Dad said, "No, you cannot do that." So we entered New York, turned around, and went back to New Jersey. By now, it was 3:00 a.m. and I told Nancy to call her host family. We found a payphone and called her host. The husband answered the phone and said, "I'm just getting up for my milk route. Stay where you are. I'll meet you and lead you home." I was never so happy to see a milkman in my whole life. He drove us to his home, and I walked Nancy up to the side door of the house. Nancy was feeling very low and sad. She thought that she would never see me again. She felt like this whole debacle was her fault. She put her head down as she said good night. I gently lifted her chin and gave her a two-second kiss with deep feelings. It was a kiss that neither one of us ever forgot.

The next day, we all drove back to Minnesota. I picked up Nancy and her cousin at the host family home. Everything was calm. Nancy rode in my car, and we played a traveling game called pediddle and peduncle. The first one to see a car with one headlight would shout out, "Pediddle!" If I was the one to see it first, I could kiss Nancy. And if she was the first one to see it, she could sock me in the arm. I never got socked! The same was true for a taillight that was out. Again, Nancy was intentionally slow on the draw. So more kissing ensued. The trip home was so much fun. Our budding relationship made the long trip go very quickly. On the radio, there was a song that played repeatedly, "See You in September." I remember it so clearly, and it's still in my mind. The words of this song were so haunting, because I was going off to Calvin College and Nancy was entering her junior year of high school. My fear was that we would part ways and never meet again. I didn't want to lose her to another summer love. As we all know, there is danger in a full moon on a summer night.

Dad and Mom drove me to Calvin College. My roommate's name was Ray Slagers. Ray was from New Jersey, and he was the son of a fisherman. Dean Phillip Lucas, in his infinite wisdom, created a new housing arrangement called Project V. In short, he organized one floor of our dormitory with students from all over the United States who all had the same class schedule. It was an experiment. Indeed, looking back, it was a phenomenal experience filled with wonderful friendships, and rich relationships. Shortly after this picture (cite) of Ray and me standing outside the dorm, Mom and Dad left. I cannot tell you how happy this moment was for me. *Freedom!*

Suffice it to say, there were many wonderful experiences that year. Two stand out. Paul Schrader (who later became a famous screenwriter) lived in my dormitory. I was assigned to write a paper on *The Scarlet Letter* by Nathanial Hawthorne. I had absolutely no idea what the deeper meaning of this book was. I asked Paul Schrader to help me, and he did. I was completely amazed at what the author of this book communicated. Paul Schrader opened my mind to the beauty of good literature. I stayed up all night typing my report and received an A. To be honest, that evening with Paul Schrader prompted me to become an English major. More importantly, my call to ministry was also confirmed.

The second experience was the night there was a big, bad water fight on our floor. I had exams to study for, and I went into the janitor's closet to study. You may think this is very weird and unbelievable, but in the quiet of that closet, I heard God speaking audibly, "I want you to be a minister." It was clear and distinct. I have never ever had anything like that happen to me before. And so, I name this the call of God on my life.

Freedom is a two-edged sword. In the past, I had always been a good student. But my first semester at Calvin College was a disaster. My GPA was 1.99. It took no effort to earn that, and it took a lot of effort to improve it! I was simply having too much fun. My second semester, I was on probation. It was good that I was put on probation because I knew that I had to work very hard for the rest of my college years. Bringing up a bad GPA is very, very difficult. I'm happy to report that I did graduate with a B-plus average.

I must now tell you about my good friend, Ron Polinder. Ron was from Lynden, Washington; he was also part of Project V on the second floor of VanderWerp dormitory. At our freshman orientation, we all went to the beach at Holland, Michigan and played football. Ron was a big man, six three and at least two hundred pounds. He was on the opposing team. I wore glasses, and he called me, "Four eyes."

I said, "Don't call me four eyes again." He did it again. I took him by the collar and took him down. This was unexpected, as I was a skinny little guy, six one and about 150 pounds.

I got him on the ground and put my knee on his chest. I said, "Don't call me four eyes ever again!" In some miraculous way, that moment bonded us. We became good friends and still are to this day.

In our sophomore year, we rented an upstairs room together. The landlord's name was Ron Vanden Bosch. His home was close to the Franklin campus of Calvin College. Often at night, we would get so hungry that we'd flip a coin to see who would go down and steal food from his refrigerator. One night, Ron and I had a tremendous water fight. I was walking down the stairs, and he dumped a whole bucket of water on my head. That was testing the limits of Ron Vanden Bosch's patience. He confronted both of us for our delinquent behavior and for stealing his food. We never did either of those behaviors again. It was during this time that Ron broke up with his girlfriend Coleen. They were engaged. He came home one night, threw her ring on his bed, and said, "I'm done with Coleen." I told him that was a stupid thing to do. To this day, I'm not exactly sure what happened with their romance. Ron did date other women. He soon came to his senses, and eventually they reunited. Ron married Coleen after his junior year at Calvin. He wanted me to be in his wedding the summer of 1967. I really wanted to go to Lynden, Washington; I was honored to be asked to be one of his groomsmen. Faye said that I needed to work and couldn't go. I regret not going to the wedding. It still pains me. Of course, Ron was very gracious. He said he understood. Ron's beautiful wife Coleen passed away from brain cancer after their children were grown. Ron happily remarried a wonderful woman named Judy. They live in Lynden, Washington. We reconnected at our fifty-year college reunion in 2018. We had a splendid and memorable time together.

To my great relief, Nancy and I wrote love letters for two years. Nancy was taking French in high school. When she would sign her letters, she would close in French. I was hoping it would say love. I went to the French professor, and I asked what each signature meant. To my great dismay, it was never love! She was very cagey and clever. I so wanted to hear the word *love*. When she graduated from high school in 1966, Nancy said that I convinced her to attend Calvin College. In my junior year, Nancy came to Calvin College to pursue a degree in nursing. My life was complete. My true love was in the dorm at Knollcrest, and I was a dorm counselor at Franklin campus. Knollcrest and Franklin campus were about five miles apart. The distance was probably a good thing as we both had to study hard.

During my senior year, I was the staff advisor at the Franklin men's dorm. I resided in a very large room on the first floor of the dorm. My room was adjacent to the dorm mother, Mrs. Kerner. Nancy was now living in the dormitory at Blodgett Hospital, where she was in her junior year of nursing. Nancy would often walk to Franklin, which was about two miles away from Blodgett. It was during this year that our love deepened, and it became clearer that we had a future together. Nancy's mother said they would not pay for her tuition if we married before her graduation.

This is the best time to provide you with events that were happening with Mom and Dad Evenhuis. In 1967, I was a junior at Calvin College. I was informed that Dad had suffered a minor stroke while pastoring in Pease, Minnesota. Dad's cardiologist recommended that Dad move to a warmer climate. Since Faye's brother, Jerome, and his family lived in Buena Park, California became their logical choice for their move.

In June of 1968, I graduated from Calvin College. I wish it was a bigger deal, but it wasn't. I only remember graduating and having lunch with my adopted brother John, Gayle, and Nancy. I then got on an airplane to live in California with my parents. It was a historic and tumultuous year as Bobby Kennedy and Martin Luther King were both assassinated. After my summer in California, I returned to Grand Rapids. In September of 1968, I started my first year at Calvin Seminary. I was also the staff advisor at Boer/Bennick dormitory, which was the first coed housing at Calvin College. By this time, Nancy and I were engaged. My proposal was surprisingly unromantic. We went to Dekker Jewelry to look at rings; my uncle Harvey was a jeweler. He picked out a diamond ring, placed it on Nancy's finger. It fit perfectly. I said, "You might as well keep it as you're going to get it sooner or later." It was there that I asked her to marry me, and she said yes. Uncle Harvey was our witness. I thought that Calvin Seminary would just be a continuation of my positive years at Calvin College. Much to my disappointment, the atmosphere at seminary was highly competitive, intellectual, and dry. I was bored and stagnating. Never once did I feel this oppression at Calvin College. I said to myself, *I'm simply going to tough it out for three years, graduate, and change the church.* Dream on Eric!

After my first year at seminary, we made plans to get married June 21, 1969. I couldn't wait. The day June 21 was my reason to live. Following my first year in seminary, I traveled to Minnesota for the wedding at Nancy's church in Renville, Minnesota. Of course, I asked my dad to perform the ceremony. I asked my adopted brother John to be my best man. Many of our college friends attended our wedding. It was a really meaningful event. Following the rehearsal at church, we went to Nancy's home. Nancy's family always provided fun, food, and laughter. Nancy's mom and Aunt Grace tap-danced to *East Side West Side*. Everyone had a fun evening except for Faye. On the evening of the wedding rehearsal, Nancy looked stunningly beautiful. She was wearing a white eyelet, empire dress with a pink ribbon. Faye said to my dad, Robert, that her skirt was too short and the neckline was too low. So Dad pulled Nancy aside and said, "Now that you're going to be a minister's wife you can't dress this way. The skirt's too short, and neckline's too low." Of course, Nancy was hurt and embarrassed. To add insult to injury, Faye also instructed Dad to warn us of the evils of dancing, movies, and card playing in his wedding message. Unfortunately, he did it! It was inappropriate for the wedding ceremony. This was our special day, which we had been anticipating for a long time. Faye had the unique ability to take the shine off our special day.

Nevertheless, it was a great wedding. The reception was held in the fellowship hall of the church. We ate ham, buns, fruit salad, and a beautiful wedding cake by Loretta Mulder (Dorothy's cousin). That evening we traveled to Brainerd, Minnesota, for our honeymoon at a famous resort on a lake. Every day it rained, except one day when I tried to teach Nancy how to golf. The golf lesson was not a success. (In fact, to this day, she hates to have me tell her how to golf.)

Following our honeymoon, we moved to Minneapolis where I had a summer assignment at Faith Christian Reformed Church in New Brighton, Minnesota. During that summer, there were two memorable events. One was my first sermon ever on Psalm 23. The supervising minister said to me, "If all else fails, just read your sermon." I think it went pretty well. The second memorable event that summer was when an American landed on the moon. I vividly remember watching this event at the home of our new friends Ron and June Taylor. History was happening right before our eyes.

After my summer assignment, we returned to Grand Rapids for my second year of studies. It was still stale and boring. Nancy now was working at Pine Rest Christian Hospital. She had achieved passing her nursing boards! And this was her first job as a registered nurse. My very good friend Jerry Alferink recommended to me that I take a summer of clinical pastoral education at Pine Rest. At first, I resisted as I simply wanted to graduate from seminary and move on with my career. However, Nancy said that I would really enjoy the hospital.

And so I followed their good advice. I signed up for a summer clinical pastoral education (CPE) program and was accepted. Reverend Jim Kok was the newly appointed CPE supervisor at Pine

Rest. Nancy and I rented a small house about a mile away from the hospital. The rent was eighty-five dollars a month!

After the death of my mother Evelyn, I had never told anyone about my past. I had told Nancy, but other than immediate family, this was a secret. The reason I kept this a secret was because I could. My adopted father, Robert, was a very prestigious pastor in the Christian Reformed Church. In addition, he was also well-respected at Calvin College and Seminary. Because of his position in the church, my past was never questioned; I never volunteered any of this sordid information.

Up until the time of my training at Pine Rest Christian Hospital, I had not been confronted to tell the truth of my story. Had these childhood events happened today, I would have been placed in grief therapy. To be honest, I had never psychologically dealt with the many tragic and difficult events in my life. Therefore, all of these thoughts and feelings were bound up in me as if they were in a safe deposit box at a bank.

In one of our first therapy sessions, the good Reverend Jim Kok said, "So, Eric, what's up with your story?" I remember thinking, *Oh my! What am I going to share?* For the first time in a long time, I told the truth. It wasn't easy. There was a point in that summer when I felt like I was going psychotic because I was finally dealing with the truth.

As I look back on that summer now, I was beginning to process the pain of my past. It was a past that I had repressed, and was now exploring. The pain was so intense that I didn't know how to process it. But thanks to God, I had my dear wife who listened with deep compassion for me. I knew Jim Kok also cared deeply for me. I now have great respect for mental health professionals, who supported me at Pine Rest Christian Hospital. They not only supported me, but they gave me hope that I could be a normal and an effective person in my calling as a pastor. One of my new revelations and insights was that there were strong Christian professionals who were very intellectual. They were genuine and approachable human beings. As a result of this wonderful summer, I applied and was accepted to be a chaplain intern at Pine Rest for one year. In that one year, I earned four more units of CPE under the remarkable supervision of Reverend Jim Kok. During that year, I became a very good friend of Reverend Jim Kok. He loved, supported, accepted, and encouraged me, and he became a role model of kindness and compassion. There will never be another Jim Kok. We are still really good friends to this day.

After having many wonderful experiences at Pine Rest with both staff and patients, I can say that it was a turning point for my personal and professional life. Pine Rest opened up new doors to various types of ministry. So in the fall of 1971, I returned to Calvin Seminary with a new and refreshed spirit. It was now my final year at the seminary. Much to my surprise, I really enjoyed my final year of seminary. It wasn't the seminary that changed, though. It was me.

In the winter of 1971, I was working as a chaplain at Pine Rest. While living in California, Dad was told that he could resume full-time ministry, and he did receive a call to Rehoboth Christian Reformed Church in Bellflower, California. But it wasn't long after he accepted this call that Dad experienced more health problems. He required open-heart surgery at St. Vincent's Hospital in Los Angeles. Sadly, Dad's repair failed, and he required a second surgery the same day. This meant that he would have to retire permanently. My adopted brother, John, and I flew to California to be with our father.

Now I want to tell you about my classmate Bryce Mensink. In the final year of seminary, there are both written and oral examinations. Bryce Mensink was in my study group of six fellow students. One night, we were studying for these examinations. We were all exhausted! It was about one o'clock in the morning when we finished our studying. I remember Bryce lying in the gutter and saying, "Even if my life ended in the gutter, God would still love me." It was his attempt at being humorous, and for me, it was a teaching moment of God's grace. The reason I mention this is because Bryce told me to continue my graduate studies at a seminary that would qualify me for a doctoral degree and a licensed counseling degree. I will never forget his advice.

I checked out Fuller Theological Seminary in Pasadena, California. Fuller Seminary offered the perfect program. I could get a doctor of ministry degree, and a master's degree in marriage and family therapy. I applied for this program and was accepted. There were two professors at Fuller Seminary who were both Calvin Seminary graduates. They also knew of my father, Reverend Robert Evenhuis. The first was Dr. Lewis Smedes, professor of ethics. The second was Dr. James Daane, professor of preaching. Dr. Daane was also the gatekeeper for doctoral students at Fuller. I was interviewed and soon informed that I was accepted in the doctor of ministry program.

The summer after I graduated from Calvin Seminary, Nancy and I traveled to Estes Park, Colorado. There I worked as a minister for the Rocky Mountain National Park ministry. This was a most magnificent and awe-inspiring experience. I led Sunday morning worship for the campers. As the worship service began, we were beside a beautiful bubbling brook with wild flowers in the meadow and snow-capped mountains in the background against azure blue skies. I opened the worship service with these beautiful words, "The Lord is in his holy temple, let all the earth keep silence before Him." And then there was a brief inspiring moment of silence!

While in Colorado, we learned that Nancy was pregnant! Wow! What a spectacular surprise. We knew that we were moving to California. We both were very excited about our pregnancy and the move. We then packed up a small U-Haul and drove to California. Once there, we needed a place to live. We looked in classified ads and found an opportunity to be apartment managers close to Fuller Seminary. I called the owner and told him that we were "very dependent and reliable." I meant to say dependable. His name was Gus Hilbert, and his wife was Lota. She was a lovely lady and very excited about our anticipated baby. We interviewed. They hired us giving us free rent. Being an apartment manager gave us many eye-opening experiences.

Grad school was new to me. I knew I had to take classes and write a dissertation to graduate. Coming from a very authoritarian style of education, I thought that Fuller would tell me what to write about. When I first met Dr. Robert Bower, it was quite intimidating. He was a very nice man with a big office and books all around. I was thinking that he would give me an assignment to write my dissertation. I was wrong. He told me I could write about anything I wanted to, as long as he approved my proposal. I couldn't believe the freedom granted to me to write about anything that came to mind. I liked literature, poetry, and metaphors. My English major at Calvin College proved to be indispensable. All of this led me to the creative idea of writing about the marital imagery in the Old Testament and New Testament. I remembered that, in the Old Testament, God married and divorced His wife Israel. I also remembered that, in the New Testament, there was bridal imagery where Jesus is the bridegroom and the Church is the bride. I proposed to Dr. Bower that my dissertation would be "Marital Reconciliation under the Analogy of Christ and the Church." He approved my proposal.

I loved doing all the research on this topic. Suffice it to say, I wrote about the marriage between God and Israel. This marriage ended in disillusionment and divorce. Thanks to God, there is a new bridal imagery in the New Testament. This new marriage fit perfectly with the theories of Hobart Mowrer, called "integrity therapy." I loved everything about Fuller Seminary. Through my many meetings with Dr. Robert Bower, we became dear friends. My desire to honor him fueled my completion of my dissertation.

But the most blessed event at Fuller was the birth of our precious Tera Lynn. On Wednesday morning, February 14, 1973, Nancy was in the bathtub, trying to soothe her cramps, as she thought this wasn't the real deal.

I began timing her "cramps." I said, "These are contractions, and we are going to the hospital." I raced to Arcadia Methodist Hospital, hoping to get stopped by the Pasadena police. I didn't know exactly where to go, so we parked in the front of the hospital. We began a slow walk up a long sidewalk to the entrance. Whenever Nancy had a contraction, we had to stop walking. Along this sidewalk was a glass stairwell that went up to the top floor of the hospital. This was at shift change, so by the time we reached the entrance, every floor had nurses watching to see if we were going to make it. At the end of the walk, we were met by a medical staff person with a wheelchair. They wheeled Nancy right up to the obstetric ward, and Tera Lynn was born before 11:00 a.m. that day. A healthy, darling little girl. Not only was she a treasure, but a love because she was born on Valentine's Day! What a gift from God, and she still blesses us today! My father baptized Tera Lynn. He said she would be filled with the Holy Spirit her whole life. How right he was!

The remainder of our days at Fuller were filled with hard work, joy, and happiness. I finished my dissertation and all of my course work at Fuller and North Hollywood Family Study Center. I then put myself up for a call to a ministry in the Christian Reformed Church. As God in His providence would have it, I received a call from Christ Community Church in Spring Lake, Michigan. It was Reformed Church.

We prayed, and I accepted this call as youth minister in a team ministry. It was a dynamic, growing church. When I told my dad I had accepted a call in the Reformed Church, he said, "What is this nonsense about you going to the Reformed Church?" I said, "It's all part of God's providential plan." The Christian Reformed Church and the Reformed Church are two different denominations and, in the past, experienced theological rivalries. Dad was born and raised in the Christian Reformed Church and gave the best years of his life as a pastor there. He was completely loyal, dedicated, and loved the church. I fully understood his comment.

This is my roommate, Ray Slagers, and me on my first day at Calvin College.

Nancy Watson finally arrived at Calvin College in the fall of 1966. Such a beauty.

Ron Polinder, who became my best
friend at Calvin College

This picture is taken at Dekkers Jewelry in Zeeland,
Michigan where I proposed to Nancy in May of 1968.

Nancy's graduation from Blodgett
Memorial Hospital School of Nursing

A very cute picture of Nancy's
youngest sister, Peggy Watson

This is a photograph of Peggy and Nancy taken in 1969.

This is a picture of Nancy's parents, Warren and
Dorothy Watson at their 25th wedding anniversary

Nancy and her parents and her sister, Peggy
on the farm in Renville, Minnesota

My graduation picture from Calvin College in 1968

My dad, Rev. Robert Evenhuis and me at our wedding

My favorite wedding picture of Nancy and me

Nancy and I leaving the church after
our wedding for our honeymoon

Our cool look in the 70's

My first quarter of Clinical Pastoral Education at Pine Rest Christian Hospital with my supervisor, Rev. James Kok is sitting to my right. This was the beginning of acknowledging the truth of my life and my mother's death and my adoption.

Tera Lynn, our first child born February 14, 1973 Valentine's Day at Arcadia Methodist Hospital, California

My father baptized Tera Lynn at the Arcadia Christian
Reformed Church. We are all admiring this new treasure

Four

༺✿༻

My Family Years (Twenty-Eight to Fifty)

T he moving van came to our apartment in Pasadena,
California, and we were on a new adventure to Spring Lake,
Michigan. In the Christian Reformed Church, I needed to
become a candidate to receive a call to ministry in a church setting.
After being in another seminary (Fuller Theological Seminary), our
denomination required me to undergo an interview by the board
of the Calvin Theological Seminary. While I was being interviewed
in Grand Rapids, Michigan, two Reformed Churches in western
Michigan expressed interest in calling me, and we arranged interviews.
I did accept a call to Christ Community Church in Spring Lake,
Michigan. Christ Community Church was a flourishing popular
church in the Spring Lake/Grand Haven area. I was called to be the
minister of youth and education, the fourth ordained pastor to join
the team ministry.

After being examined by the Reformed Church, I was duly
ordained at Christ Community Church. My ordination was glorious
and inspiring. My good friend, Reverend Jim Kok; my dear father,
Reverend Robert Evenhuis; and Reverend Richard Rhem all
participated in this service. In addition, the minister of music, Greg

Bryson, provided the most inspiring and beautiful music. The most meaningful part of this service was kneeling on the pulpit, with many pastors coming forth, and laying hands on me while my father prayed. It truly was one of the most highly spiritual moments in my life.

However, as time went on, I soon came to realize that I knew nothing about youth ministry or education. It is a terrible feeling to act as if you know what you're doing when you don't. After one year, it was clear that this was a mistake. The church was very kind; they gave me a good severance package, and we parted ways amicably. Now what to do! I had a good friend in Grand Rapids, Michigan—Dr. Doug Blocksma—who offered to supervise me and encouraged me to start my own counseling practice. Even though this was a difficult year, it was also a time of great joy when on July 20, 1974, our sweet, compliant Natalie Joy was born. Tera was a year and half, Natalie was an infant, and we were very busy! Natalie was a happy baby and found Tera's antics amusing, so there was a lot of laughter in our home.

In addition to starting my own practice of marriage and family counseling, I also was employed as a drug and alcohol counselor on the substance abuse unit at Mercy Hospital in Muskegon, Michigan. This was added value to my career. Also, I was a probation officer for the Fifty-Eighth District Court in Grand Haven, Michigan. This, too, was beneficial to my career as pastoral counselor. I found it very interesting that my pastoral identity was helpful to the people I counseled. As a pastoral counselor, I gave people a sense of confidence and hope. So even though Christ Community Church did not work out for me, God's plan for my life was fulfilled.

There were other things in Spring Lake that enhanced my life as well. When we moved there, we rented a house that the church picked out for us. It was a lovely two-story house, but it was temporary housing as we were looking to purchase our first home. Robert Hendricks showed us a really disgusting and dumpy house, but it was right on Spring Lake. He told us that, with a little elbow grease and a lot of effort, this house could increase in value quickly.

We needed Nancy's parents to loan us $10,000 as a down payment.

We showed Nancy's parents the home. Nancy's mother hated the house, and Nancy was influenced by her mother. Nancy's dad said, "They can spend the money however they want. They just have to repay us."

I said, "Let's buy the house and fix it up."

This was our first test of wills. Nancy got up late at night after arguing and said she was leaving. She drove around and then realized there was nowhere to go, so she came home, and she said, "OK, we'll buy the house." The previous owners raised Irish setters. So the house smelled of dogs. It was a mess. We rolled up our sleeves, consulted an interior decorator, and used his ideas. We learned how to wallpaper, lay carpet, and paint. The house was transformed into a lovely home on the water. Nancy even made the curtains and throw pillows. Now Nancy's mother, after seeing the transformation, was very pleased. Still, she was worried that our children, her grandchildren, would drown. Our front lawn ended at the water with a four-foot seawall. So Nancy's parents helped build a fence around the entire front yard to protect Tera and Natalie. Nancy coached Tera if she ever fell into the water to swim to the ladder hold on, and yell, "Help, help, help!" as loudly as possible. The next day, she quizzed Tera and asked what to do if she fell in, and she replied, "Drown." It made us laugh but also made us worry. Tera Lynn was a strong-willed child, and Natalie was very compliant. Nancy read a book, *The Strong-Willed Child* by James Dobson. Natalie asked Nancy why she was reading the book, and Nancy said, "It's a book about your sister."

Since we lived on the lake, we soon purchased a twenty-three-foot, single-mast sailboat with our very good friends Rod and Cheryl Van Abbema. We moored the sailboat in front of our home, and the boat gave us many wonderful and harrowing experiences.

We sailed to Saugatuck with more good friends, Tom and Bev Elzinga. On the trip, we ended up in a deep fog and were headed straight for the beach when another boat came out of the fog and yelled, "Hard starboard!" an urgency that made us immediately obey. We eventually made it into safe harbor, only to secure a slip for the night. The harbormaster said, "We don't rent slips to transients." But when he saw Nancy and Bev, he said, "Oh, you guys are all right." It pays to marry up. We were secure for the night.

On another occasion, as we were sailing, Tera said in great terror, "It's tipping!" I replied, "Tera, it's not tipping. It's heeling." This did little to relieve her fears. Nevertheless, the boat was a huge part of our enjoyment and adventure of living in Spring Lake. Sailing was terrific in the summers of 1974–1977.

In Spring Lake, the girls went from infancy to preschool. So potty training, talking, walking, and riding big wheels! Nancy worked at Mercy Hospital, two days a week. We hired Mrs. Olthoff to care for the girls when we worked. She was nurturing and had a great hearty laugh. She was a wonderful, positive influence, and we all loved her. In the interest of the children, I built them a nice sandbox. One day, when the children were playing in the sandbox, Tera was feeding Natalie sand. Natalie just had her mouth open. Thank God for Mrs. Olthoff, who witnessed this, rescued her, and rinsed her mouth for a long time to get rid of all the sand. It was very traumatic for Mrs. Olthoff and probably the girls as well.

Another blessing of Spring Lake was the Brown family, who lived next door. Every day, Mr. Brown had his afternoon sherry, and sometimes Nancy would join Mr. Brown and his wife for relief. Their daughter Anna was our babysitter. She was so trustworthy, and we allowed her to spend the night with Tera when Natalie was born. They all became very dear friends. Their younger two children, Deidre and Jimmy, often came to play with the girls. Our first Halloween, Tera was in a Vikings stocking hat as her costume, and I took her to the neighbors. She was bold, and asked at each home for candy for her baby sister. Natalie wasn't even old enough to eat candy, but Tera persisted anyway.

Another interesting event was their first formal photography session. It was a sales pitch from Olin Mills, and Nancy insisted that it be taken with both girls to save money. Natalie couldn't even sit up alone, but after Nancy argued with the photographer, they finally propped Natalie up leaning on Tera and took the photograph. It's amazing how poverty can influence behavior. Another example of Nancy's frugality was Christmas dresses that she made, even embroidering a design on the pinafore. First, the blouse underneath was red gingham under a white pinafore. The next year, she added a green ruffle and made a green blouse. I believe there was a third reincarnation of this dress, but I can't remember the details.

We'll end this Spring Lake chapter with the 1978 storm of the century. Nurses were transported to the hospital on snowmobiles. When we loaded the moving van with our belongings, the snow was so high that nobody would have known that we moved, as the snowbanks were ten feet high. The economy was struggling due to challenges in the auto industry, and bumper stickers said, "The last one out of the state, turn out the lights." It was a great time to leave Michigan.

On one very cold, cloudy, and snowy day in February of 1977, Nancy said, "Don't you know somebody that could hire you, so we can move back to California?" I was able to reply to her that I knew Dr. Robert Zondervan, who was a psychiatrist with the Voorman Psychiatric Clinic. I called Dr. Zondervan, and he said the clinic was looking to hire a chaplain. As God directed, I was scheduled to give a talk in Oklahoma City for the Christian Association for Psychological Studies. I submitted my topic (my dissertation), and it was accepted by Dr. Ted Monsma. Because finances were tight, I called Dr. Monsma, and told him I could not attend this conference. He said, "Well, that really perturbs me." And then, I replied, "OK. I'll go."

Again, as God would have his way, Dr. Gary Voorman, a psychiatrist from California, attended my seminar. We had dinner together and we continued corresponding. In November of 1977, I interviewed with the staff of the Voorman Clinic. Nancy and the girls joined me, and I remember distinctly a gentleman who was a NASA engineer on the flight with us. He leaned over and said, "You're a very wealthy man." I didn't understand what he meant, as I was far from financially wealthy. But I was indeed wealthy because of my wife and two beautiful daughters. Even today, this memory touches me deeply. We went back to Michigan, not knowing our future. Then in December, we spent Christmas at Nancy's parents' home on the farm in Renville, Minnesota. I received a phone call from Dr. Voorman, informing me that he wanted to hire me as the chaplain. Nancy screamed with joy. And then she looked over and saw her mother crying, as this meant we would have to move far away from them. A new chapter was to be written.

Once again, a moving van picked up our belongings, and we went to California. I will never forget driving through Palm Springs in February of 1978. To this day, I love the green mountains capped with white snow and blue skies above. This was like a dream come true.

We were advised to purchase a home in Upland, California. It was a three-bedroom, ranch-style house. Our realtor was Vic Koning. In order to obtain the loan, we needed one hundred dollars a month more to qualify. Our hearts sank, but Mr. Koning said, "We'll talk to Dr. Voorman." I remember nervously meeting in Dr. Voorman's office, and Mr. Koning said, "Eric needs one hundred dollars more in his salary." I remember Dr. Voorman said, "This is the first time I gave someone a raise before they even started working." Nancy gave Dr. Voorman a big hug, and the house was ours. It was a happy house to raise our daughters.

One of the conditions for employment was to become a clinical pastoral education supervisor (CPE). I already had six units of basic CPE under my belt. The next step in the process was to participate in supervisory CPE. I did this both at St. Joseph Hospital in Orange, California, under supervision of George Markum, and at Loma Linda University Medical Center under supervision of Jerry Davis. I then became an acting supervisor of CPE. This allowed me to supervise seminary students and pastors at Horizon Psychiatric Hospital. Dr. Gary Voorman was the medical director at Horizon Hospital. He knew I needed an office to supervise students. He gave me the biggest office in the hospital. Not only was it the biggest, but also it was off the lobby of the entrance to the hospital. Office space is an indication of status. Part of my training required me to undergo individual therapy. My first therapist was Ellen Beauchamp. Dr. Beauchamp was a psychologist who left her calling as a nun. She was helpful to me in many ways. She knew nothing about CPE and the processes involved.

When I explained it to her, she said, "Eric, this fits perfectly into your ACA (adult child of alcoholic) pathology."

She was right. I was involved in a very rigorous and nebulous process with no guarantee of a positive outcome. In the book *Adult Children of Alcoholics* written by Janet Woititz, she writes, "Can you visualize what it was like at home? Do you remember how it felt? What did you expect when you walked in the door. You hoped that everything would be fine, but you never knew for sure. And somehow, no matter how many times you walked through the door, you never were prepared for a positive experience" And so I terminated my role as a CPE acting supervisor. I joined an ACA group therapy. Our group met every Wednesday at Lincoln Park in Pomona, California. Each week, we had a picnic and discussed the twelve-step program of ACA. To this very day, I love picnics. This group was very therapeutic and life changing. The group consisted of mental health professionals and clergy and it continued for years.

As time went on, the Voorman Clinic was in turmoil. Dr. Voorman informed me that he could no longer continue to employ me. This was very, very frightening. At the time, hospital insurance was changing. Now, in order to be paid, hospitals and professionals needed to be accepted on insurance panels that now were controlling what hospitals and doctors were to be paid, whereas in the past, insurance companies had needed to comply with whatever fees were being charged. Financial decisions needed to be made.

Even though this was an economic decision, Dr. Voorman continued to be very emotionally supportive to our family. At this time, Dr. Andy Rooks was the medical director of the hospital. Dr. Rooks was a wonderful Christian psychiatrist, and for a short period of time, he personally provided my salary to continue to be chaplain at Horizon Hospital. I could not believe his kind generosity. It was during this time that the administrator of Charter Oak Psychiatric Hospital, Barbar Noblett, invited me to be their hospital chaplain. I'm always amazed at how God provides.

DARK CLOUDS

As good as life was, a really, really dark cloud came unexpectedly. Dr. Voorman often said, "Before the death of a loved one, there usually is a wonderful, positive event." And, how true this proved to be for me. We celebrated Mother's Day on May 9 of 1982, at our home in Upland. We enjoyed a wonderful time with Mom and Dad Evenhuis. I vividly remember making pineapple bowls with maraschino cherries with little toothpicks. After lunch, we had a robust game of badminton. Dad loved to play badminton. He went to hit the birdie, and he fell hard on his back. So the game ended, but the day was 100 percent positive. Tuesday May 11, Mom and Dad drove to see Dad's sister, Martha, who lived in Redwood City, California. On Mother's Day, he told me that he wanted to share the gospel of Jesus Christ with Martha. As they were approaching King City on Highway 101, Mom was driving. Dad stiffened up, and Mom hit him hard on his chest as she drove. He said, "I must have had a spell." Mom pulled over to the side of the road and put Dad in the back seat of the car, and she continued to drive a brief way to the King City exit. Dad's last words to Mom were, "I think this is it." Mom frantically drove to Bob's Big Boy, just off the exit. Just as she ran into the restaurant, a local medical doctor was leaving and told Mom to follow him to King City hospital. This was a few blocks away. At the hospital, they did try to revive Dad, but were unsuccessful. My precious father, Robert Evenhuis, died in the back seat of the car. My mother called Horizon Hospital and asked for me. My secretary, Diana Koning, answered the call and said, "He is having lunch at the Institute of Iniquity." It was supposed to be the Institute of Antiquity, with Dr. Marvin Meyer. Mom did indeed tell Diana that my father had passed away. When I returned to the hospital, Dr. Rooks, Dr. Voorman, and Dr. Smith were all with me as they informed me of Dad's passing. It was shocking and unbelievable. My mother needed me. Of course, I called Nancy and told her the bad news. We made arrangements for me to fly to San Jose, and the minister from San Jose Christian Reformed Church drove me to the hospital in King City to meet my mom and drive her home. I arrived around midnight. I drove Mom home to our Upland home, where Nancy, Uncle Jerome, and Aunt Marge Kalmink (Mom's brother and his wife) were waiting for us. It was a surreal evening, and one I will never forget. The next day, John and Gayle flew out to California. We made arrangements for Dad's funeral at the Redlands Christian Reformed Church, where Reverend Jerry Alferink conducted Dad's funeral. The church was packed. Since Dad was to be buried in Holland, Michigan, his body was flown to Michigan where a second funeral was held at the Borculo Christian Reformed Church. Dr. Carl Kromminga conducted the service. Once again, the church was packed. Both services were a testament to the impact that his life and ministry had on so many people. And so we buried my father and returned home to California. When we returned home, Natalie, in her childlike understanding of all of this, said, "Why couldn't God have waited until after Father's Day?"

Dad's death had a profound effect on me. He gave me a great legacy, and I will be forever grateful. In that, I will never ever believe in luck. I believe with all my heart that God has a purpose for everything that happens in my life. Nothing comes to us by fate, but by God's loving, fatherly hand. Not a day goes by that I don't think about Robert. He was a good, kind, and gentle man. Dad was best known for his wonderful prayers. After his death, Faye gave me all of his recorded prayers of various worship services. I edited these prayers in my first book, *"My Father's Prayers"*.

SAILING ADVENTURES

Now I am going to take a little sidebar to fill you in on other events in my life. I still had a continued love of sailing. In addition, there were a number of injuries and accidents. These events all played a big part of my story.

Sailing has been one of my all-time passions. I knew little about sailing until Nancy suggested we buy a sixteen-foot, modified, catamaran, trailerable, sailboat. Nancy was working at Pine Rest, and one of her patients was selling this boat. Dan Vander Vliet and I decided to buy this boat together. It was in the summer of 1971 that Dan, Nancy, and I went out for our maiden sail on Reed's Lake in Grand Rapids. We were told that this boat could not flip. Well, it flipped, and the mast went straight down in the water. Dan and I were sitting on the bottom of the boat; Nancy was swimming around scooping up our wallets and other papers that were floating, and stuffing them in her bathing suit.

It was totally impossible to flip the boat upright. A nice man with a motorboat came by, and rescued us. He tied a rope under the bottom and slowly motored away. The boat was righted with the sail and mast up. The nice man towed us to shore after we lowered the sail. We then put the boat on the trailer and called it a day. That trip certainly hadn't worked out too well. Subsequent to that disastrous maiden sailing day though, we had many memorable times on the water. Sailing was a great antidepressant in my last year of seminary.

As I mentioned before, our second sailboat was a twenty-three-foot Columbia sloop that we moored at our home on Spring Lake. Again, we had many wonderful memories during out time on Spring Lake.

Upon moving to California, one of my first assignments from Dr. Voorman was to find a thirty-six-foot sloop. This was a great assignment. I did indeed find the perfect boat, a thirty-six-foot Islander with all the bells and whistles necessary for racing. The previous owner named the boat *The Big Kahuna*. Dr. Voorman changed the name to *Seek Ye One*, and let me explain the double meaning of that name. In the New Testament, Jesus said, "Seek ye first in the kingdom of God"(Matthew 6:33 NIV), and in sailing terms, "seek ye first" meant crossing the finish line first in a sailboat race. And so we had many wonderful and exciting moments on *Seek Ye One*. We raced to Ensenada. We raced to Catalina Island. One memorable trip to Catalina was with Reverend Jerry Alferink and his family. Together, there were four adults, and five children. I believe it was in the fall. We left on Wednesday, and returned Saturday. The weather in Catalina was warm, sunny, and pleasant. On Saturday morning, we saw that the winds were building, so we left early. Halfway to the mainland, the winds really picked up. I reefed the main and head sail, while Jerry was at the helm. By the time we reached Long Beach, we were in a full-blown, twenty-five-knot windstorm, and it was raining. Once we came into the breakwater, it was calm. I'll never forget Jerry, on his knees, saying a heartfelt, "Thank you, Jesus!"

It was also during this time that I established a nonprofit program entitled Homeward Bound. This program was designed to take adolescents and their parents on sailing outings. It was a lot of work for the little time that we used it. The concept was a great one, and we did help many families with difficult children. The ocean has a way of humbling even the most self-centered and prideful teenager. The program was difficult to sustain due to our distance from the ocean, and the time and money required to complete a single voyage.

When we left for Traverse City, Michigan, Dr. Voorman donated the boat to the nonprofit, and we transferred the boat to Holland, Michigan. I distinctly remember him writing me a nice note that said, "This is the end of a perfect partnership." The boat arrived in Michigan in the fall of 1993. I enlisted the help of my future son-in-law, Mark Lodewyk, to sand and prepare the bottom of the boat for paint. Then we put shrink wrap around the boat for the winter months. In the late spring of 1994, once the ice was off Lake Michigan, we sailed the boat from Holland, Michigan to Traverse City, Michigan. Sailing in freshwater was a new, refreshing, and different experience from sailing in saltwater. The weather was great, the winds were favorable, and the sun was shining. But the waters were ice cold. If there were any man-overboard events, it would have meant certain death because of the frigid temperatures in Lake Michigan. We sailed the boat into the bay of Traverse City. For two summers, we, once again, had many memorable experiences with the boat. The one that stands out for me was taking a severely handicapped woman with multiple sclerosis for a gentle afternoon sail. We needed to support her in the cockpit and be very careful with her. At the end of the sail, she stated that this had fulfilled a lifelong dream, which she never thought would be fulfilled. She was so grateful! We all ended in tears after her touching speech.

The most remarkable thing about sailing *Seek Ye One* was the many fond memories that it brought to so many people. There are memories that we have forgotten, but friends and their children will remind us of their unforgettable and unique experiences that we gave them on the water. *Seek Ye One* was truly a vessel used by God for mercy, mirth, and adventure. So when we left Traverse City for California, I decided to sell the boat.

The boat was slipped into the Traverse City marina. The boat was sold in the fall of 1995, after I left for California, to a buyer in Rochester, New York. When the sale of the boat was completed, the broker sent me the front page of the local newspaper with a photograph of the boat, leaving the slip while breaking ice in the Traverse City bay. It was the end of a great era but not the end of sailing. Our next boat was a forty-four-foot sloop donated by Dr. Robert Williams. The name of this boat was *Talisman*.

The Injury List

Making an injury list was a stroke of genius. I designed the injury list when we were on vacation with our seven grandchildren. I was amazed at how children love to tell me about their injuries and mishaps. There is indeed something healing about letting Grandpa know the most recent injury. The hurt list became a great hit.

Nancy's Ankle

The first injury was Nancy's ankle. When I was registering the boat for a sailboat race, Nancy was in the parking lot. There was rope, so she decided to show the girls how to high jump. The girls held the rope up, and Nancy ran in her brown fashion boots, jumped over the rope, and came flying down on her ankle, tearing all her tendons and ligaments. She was in pain. And the bruise went from her toes to her knee. She was on crutches for two months, waiting for it to heal.

NANCY'S COLLARBONE

The next injury was when, just as her ankle was healing, she hesitated to jump over a puddle in the street. The puddle looked innocent enough, but there was green slime underneath the water in the puddle. Our friend, Roger Rose, was trying to be helpful when he impulsively picked her up and attempted to jump over the puddle to keep Nancy from getting wet. Unfortunately, things didn't work out too well. Roger slipped in the puddle, and they both fell to the street. I was laughing, without knowing the seriousness of this accident. Nancy, with slime on her shoulder and in her hair, said, "Don't laugh. I have a broken shoulder or cracked skull. I'm going into shock." I did not laugh anymore, and we rushed Nancy to the ER. It was confirmed that she had a broken collarbone and a bump to the head. Now, another recovery period ensued.

ERIC'S BROKEN ANKLE

The next injury on the list was my broken ankle. We were leading a marriage retreat for the Bellflower Christian Reformed Church couples' club in the mountains of San Bernardino. During the afternoon break, the couples organized a volleyball game. The game was played on a very hard surface with loose gravel. I was playing forward by the net and made a tremendous spike—only to come down on the hard ground, snapping my left ankle. It was a compound fracture, with the bone sticking out of the skin. The ambulance came, and I vividly remember the ambulance driver saying there were three choices of equal distance away. I said, "Take me to Loma Linda University." The trip down the mountain was extremely painful, and every bump and turn caused a jolt of severe pain. Once in the ER, I was not given any pain medicine until the doctor arrived. The doctor was Dr. Christopher Jobe, a really great orthopedic doctor. Once he arrived, they gave me pain medicine. He was talking to me nonchalantly; he suddenly jerked my ankle and put it back into reasonable alignment. He told me he had the same injury while skiing in Switzerland. They subsequently took me into surgery and placed a plate and screws to secure the bones. I had an immediate positive bond with Dr. Jobe. This injury was very serious, and I milked it for everything I could. It was very easy for me to ask my friend to put another log on the fire. It was easy for me to ask Nancy for the remote. My recovery was long and painful, but it was successful.

Nancy's Operation

Next on the injury list was Nancy's cyst on her ovary. She was having a variety of symptoms, and finally an OB/GYN doctor, Dr. Michael Rosenthal, determined this situation required immediate surgery. Nancy's parents came from Arizona and stayed a month to help because I was still on crutches; I couldn't drive my stick shift to go to work. Nancy's total hysterectomy remedied the symptoms, which all related to endometriosis. A memory I have of this event is that I was walking down the hospital hall on crutches with Nancy when the nurse asked, "Which one of you is the patient?"

Nancy's parents were a tremendous help during this trying time. We learned how *not* to comfort others in times like this. Our neighbor Kathy came over the night prior to the surgery, and said, "I had a friend who had the same thing, and she died." This was not helpful, and it raised all of our anxiety.

Tera's Knee Surgery

The next major injury was Tera's knee. She was playing soccer on a very uneven soccer field at Ontario Christian. I was not present, but Nancy was there. Tera was running down the field, and she stepped into a hole (or her toe caught behind some obstacle.) She fell and

Nancy knew immediately it was a serious injury. Natalie was also playing, and both Natalie and Tera heard the knee snap.

Nancy took her to ER, where I met them, and Dr. Goldman did surgery; he even came out of surgery to ask permission to open up the knee as he thought he could repair the torn cartilage. But after the surgery, he informed us the tear was too large, and she would eventually need another knee surgery to repair the snapped ACL (anterior cruciate ligament) in the middle of the knee. Tera's recovery was painful, and it took a long time. Her soccer career was adversely affected. Sadly, she never played with the same confidence.

ERIC AND NANCY'S SAILBOAT INJURIES

Next on the injury list was our infamous Catalina trip for Natalie's birthday, and this included three of her girlfriends. The trip was fabulous, with thousands of dolphins swimming alongside our sailboat. Since it was summer, all the moorings inside Catalina harbor were occupied. So we needed to anchor in Descanso Bay, which I called Disgusto Bay because the problem with anchoring is that all the boats move in various directions due to the wind and currents. It is very easy to get tangled up with another boat's anchor lines. Descanso Bay is a goldmine for scuba divers to bring up anchors that were severed by their owners, when tangled with another boat line.

We rented a room on the island, and the plan was for Nancy and the girls to stay in the room while I stayed on the boat. During the evening watch, I was running back and forth to ensure the anchor held, and I slipped and sprained my ankle. Now I was incapacitated to stand in the forward hatch to check the movement of the boat. Two other sailors came to our rescue and secured the anchor. I didn't trust their work, so I made Nancy check our position throughout the night. This meant that Nancy had to stand up and poke her head through the forward hatch. We were sleeping in the V-berth, which is a section of the bow of the boat. On Nancy's final check, a small piece of the V-berth gave way, and she fell to the lower level of the boat. This accident caused her great pain in her midsection. The next morning, we took a taxi boat and then a taxi to the little hospital in Catalina. They took X-rays and determined that Nancy's ribs were broken and my ankle had a severe sprain. But the more distressing part of this hospital visit was the intense questioning of us by the hospital staff. I think they thought we were in a tremendous fight and caused these injuries in the midst of a marital argument.

After we were released, we picked up the girls and their friends, and motored back to Long Beach. The girls had to manage the vessel. This was a long, slow trip without wind, which meant the trip took about six hot hours. It was another lesson to learn.

NATALIE'S BURNT QUESADILLA

We were skiing in Steamboat Springs, Colorado. We received a call from Natalie. She said, "Don't get mad," as she quietly cried, "but I set the kitchen on fire." She was fixing a quesadilla and heating the oil in a frying pan, but she forgot about it when she was interrupted by a man coming to pick up her car. She had been in a minor accident, and he was going to repair the vehicle. She decided to shower after giving him the keys, and suddenly in the shower, she remembered her hot oil. By the time she went back into the kitchen, she couldn't see through the living room due to heavy black smoke. When Tera came home, she saw Natalie with a black face from the soot, and there were streaks where her tears ran down. The blessing was that we were far away. Therefore, we could be philosophical about it. We were thankful they were safe. Nancy always said, "You are more valuable than whatever you broke." But she did tell Natalie, "Girl, this time you're pushing it!" We did receive an insurance check for the smoke damage. Natalie helped Nancy clean everything as good as new. It was a lot of work, and we had just redecorated the house, added wallpaper, new drapes, and new furnishings, which all had to be professionally cleaned.

TERA AND NATALIE'S CAR ACCIDENT

The next injury was on St. Patrick's Day. The girls were going to a St. Patrick's Day party, and I told them that tonight the Dutch, Germans, French, and especially the Irish will all be drinking tonight, so please be careful. However, as they were coming home, they were broadsided by a local restaurant manager who ran a red light. They were driving an Acura Integra, and their friend Alicia was in the back seat of the car. The accident happened about a half a mile from our home. Nancy and I heard sirens; but we didn't think much of it until we received a call from Alicia that our girls were in an accident on the corner of San Antonio and Foothill. Nancy and I drove to the scene of the accident. It reminded me of the movie *Die Hard*, with police, ambulance, and fire trucks all present. And there on the ground, were our two precious daughters lying on the backboard with white neck braces on. A policeman told me I could not enter the scene. I said, "These are my daughters, and I'm going to them." Both girls immediately said, "Dad, we're OK." I said, "Good", and then told the policeman I wanted the driver of the truck that hit them tested for drugs and alcohol. There were many witnesses that could testify that the truck driver ran a red light. Thank God there weren't any major injuries. The little red Acura was totaled. Nancy wanted to rush to her daughters but also wanted to be obedient. She was shaking. A fireman put her in the cab of the fire truck and told her to stay put. The girls were taken to ER at San Antonio Community Hospital, but were treated and released without serious injuries. Thank God for His providential care.

ERIC'S CAR ACCIDENT

In keeping with our injury list, there was one more that occurred in the next chapter of our life in 1998. I was driving home from my office in Upland on Arrow Highway. I was at a complete stop, waiting for the red light to change, and without any warning, I was rear-ended by another car that was going extremely fast. I hit the car in front of me, and that car was pushed into the car in front of her. It was a four-car accident all caused by one speeding physician who was driving a big Mercedes Benz. When he hit me, my head hit the windshield. When my car hit the car in front of me, the airbag went off. I went forward and backward, and then again forward and backward. The airbag was pure white with lots of white powder. I thought I was on my way to heaven. And then I soon realized— I was still in this world. As hard as my car had been hit, I thought the gas tank could explode. I released my seat belt and got out of the car. I looked back at the guy who hit me, and I said, "What in the world were you doing?"

The older lady in front of me was very upset. The person in front of her was upset. I walked over to the curb and sat down. A very nice man came out of the house and asked if I wanted to sit in a lawn chair. I said yes. Nancy was working at City of Hope, so I called her sister Peggy. Peggy came to the scene immediately. The police asked me a number of questions. They offered a ride in an ambulance, but since Peggy was there, she drove me to the emergency room. My left wrist was burned from the exploding air bag. My head hurt from hitting the windshield, and my shoulder was in extreme pain from the seat belt. I am not a good patient. Nancy arrived while I was in ER I was in great pain. I was demanding Demerol. They did not give it to me, as they were waiting to determine my injuries. After they bandaged the burn on my wrist, they gave me muscle relaxants, anti-anxiety medication, Vicodin, and then they sent me home.

I hired a lawyer, and the insurance companies fought it out. I did make another appointment with Dr. Christopher Jobe, and he did arthroscopic surgery on my shoulder. He said that before I die, I will need two shoulder replacements. We went to court. All in all, it was a very stressful and long recovery. This completes our major injury list.

HOSPITAL TRANSITIONS

In 1988, moving from one hospital to another is not an easy transition. I moved from being a chaplain at Horizon Hospital in

Pomona to a chaplain at Charter Oak Hospital in Covina. There are a lot of politics involved in transitions. Horizon Hospital was in turmoil, economically and politically. On the other hand, Charter Oak Hospital was a more stable and better-managed hospital. Many of the good professionals from Horizon Hospital left for Charter Oak Hospital. My favorites were Marie Carrie, who was the director of nursing, and Jackie Coyle, who was the assistant director of nursing. These two women were always supportive of my role as chaplain. It was at this time I met and became good friends with Dr. John Ursino, a psychiatrist who was from New Jersey. We developed a close working relationship and developed a relatively large counseling center in Upland, California named Magnolia Counseling Center. I would do chaplaincy work at the hospital in the morning and then see private clients in the afternoon. The schedule was manageable, and life was good. But as time went on, Charter Oak Hospital was in crisis due to HMOs (health maintenance organizations) entering the financial side of the picture. Everyone needed to be on an HMO panel. If you were not on the panel, insurance companies would not pay you. Financial life became difficult for hospitals and private practitioners. As a result, I was fired and rehired seven times by various Charter Oak Hospital administrators. Administrators were hired and fired on a regular basis. In summary, it was a very volatile time.

Hospitals were struggling. Nevertheless, my private practice was booming. Of course, this was also true for psych hospitals throughout the nation. Bethesda Christian Hospital was looking to expand their outpatient programs. I received a phone call from Bethesda Hospital in Denver, Colorado. They, too, were struggling and were hoping to establish a Christian satellite office in Southern California. They offered to buy our practice. After negotiations, we came to an agreement. The agreement was to hire me as director of the counseling center, and continue exactly as before.

When I told Nancy about this arrangement, she said I should draw up legal documents with a law firm. I am a trusting soul, but I agreed with Nancy, and a legal document was drafted. In 1992, I came back from a week's vacation, and my secretary said there was a letter from Bethesda, but I shouldn't open it right away. I said, "What?" and I disobeyed and opened the letter. They let me go as director and stopped paying the buyout. Nancy was right again. The lawyer sent a harshly worded letter to Bethesda, and they agreed to complete the payments outlined in the terms of the buyout. I was now required to find a new office, and life was uncertain and unsettled. Nancy was working at City of Hope. And there were also troubling times at her work, as the nurses' union had gone on strike.

BLUE SKIES SHINING ON ME: GEORGE AND PEGGY'S WEDDING

As difficult as this time was, there was a bright and shining moment on the horizon. A major part of family life was Nancy's precious sister, Peggy. Peggy is six years younger than Nancy. Peggy loved soft things and animals. She was loved by the extended family as well as our family. In 1972, she married Larry Eechoff, but unfortunately, the marriage ended in divorce. Peggy had an associate degree in nursing. In 1979, she moved to California and lived with us for two months. It was during this time that she met George Trindle, and they were to be married in 1986. I had the honor of marrying them on a beautiful, large, old sailboat in San Pedro Harbor. I offered one of my chaplain interns to provide music for the wedding. The only song they knew was "Knights in White Satin." They played it over and over again. It was live music, but we would have liked some variety. Nevertheless, it was a grand event. Tera and Natalie had tuxedo tee shirts, and served hors d'oeuvres. Mom and Dad Watson came from Minnesota. We were happy, as the Trindles chose to live in Upland near us, so it added greatly to our family life. To add to our joy, they quickly started a family. They had Andrew, Ashley, and Jessica. They all came quite quickly. Ross was the son of George and his ex-wife, and he joined the family at age twelve. We loved having them nearby. This was a happy occasion for us all.

Big Trouble in TRAVERSE City

In 1993, there were riots in Los Angeles because of the Rodney King verdict where LA police were found innocent. In Upland, we could even smell the smoke from buildings set on fire during the riots. We watched horrific scenes on the evening news. The most disturbing incident was when an innocent truck driver was taken from his cab and beaten almost to death. Bethesda Hospital was in crisis, because of the beginning of managed care and the large turnover of administrative staff. And Nancy's labor disputes at City of Hope led us to the possibility of moving out of California. We found an opportunity to begin in Traverse City, Michigan. There was an opportunity to begin a counseling center at Fellowship Christian Reformed Church in Traverse City, Michigan.

It had been a long time since I had been employed in a church setting. This opportunity seemed to be God's calling on our life. Nancy and I visited Traverse City, and I knew the pastor, Reverend John DeBruyn. I was a staff advisor when he was a student at Calvin College. I liked John, and we seemed a good fit. Nancy also felt this was God's calling for a new chapter in our lives. As she was struggling with this idea of a big change, she heard the scripture which says, "He who leaves father, mother, sister and brother and houses for my sake, will be rewarded in this life and the life to come" (Matthew 19:29 NIV). It felt like a voice from God. And she decided she was willing to make the big change. As I look back on this decision to accept this call to Traverse City, I believe with all my heart that this was indeed God's calling for our lives and my career. The first year in Traverse City was fantastic. We celebrated our twenty-fifth anniversary.

Tera Lynn and Marc's Wedding

We celebrated Tera's marriage to Marc de Falkenberg. We celebrated the birth of our first grandchild, Austin Taylor. We celebrated Tera's graduation from Calvin College. Tera's wedding was a spectacular event. She and Marc were married on November 5, 1994. We searched high and low for a wedding venue. After a long search, we all agreed that the wedding would take place at Calvin Seminary Chapel. This was the location of my first preaching as a student. It was also a sacred place, where I experienced many wonderful and inspiring seminary worship services. Tera was a beautiful, glowing bride. Marc was a very distinguished-looking groom. I walked Tera down the aisle with great pride. Marc's father, Robert, had the honor of opening the wedding ceremony. His remarks were heartfelt, and full of love. He mentioned that this was a "bittersweet moment for him." On the one hand, he was letting his son take another step into the natural process of adulthood. On the other hand, he was extremely pleased to welcome Tera into their family. After Robert's remarks, he asked, "Who gives this woman to this man?"

I responded, "Her mother and I." I proceeded to bring Tera to Marc. I performed the ceremony with joy and gratitude. I reminded everyone of Tera's baptism. Her grandfather had said she would be filled with the Holy Spirit her whole life. I also mentioned that Tera forgives quickly. Indeed, both of these truths reflect her character. A great reception was held nearby at an Italian restaurant. Tera has always been known as the "dancing queen." The reception was a great celebration with delicious food and a night of dancing. Despite the fact that it was a cold, rainy evening, it didn't dampen anyone's spirit for a meaningful wedding celebration.

DISILLUSIONMENT

We celebrated Natalie's first years at Calvin College. But little did we know that there were dark and ominous storm clouds forming in the future. The second year at Traverse City was the worst and most disillusioning of my entire life. Without getting into details, I became a whistleblower to abuse of power. Let me tell you that there is no joy in being a whistleblower. We blew the whistle. The church, the classis, and the denomination were all a huge disappointment.

By God's providence, Nancy got a job offer back at City of Hope as a nurse for cancer patients on a telephone service called Cancer Connection. Her sister Peggy helped her obtain this job. Nancy told Peggy she was waiting for God to give direction. Peggy replied, "I am God, and you must take this job and live in our home until Eric can join you." This was a welcome direction.

In 1994, we purchased a beautiful house overlooking Traverse East Bay. I had decided to split the three-acre plot. I wanted to keep one and half acre for a future home to be built. I stayed behind to finish up my counseling practice and oversee the property. One of the most beautiful experiences was being the spiritual leader for Walk to Emmaus weekend. This was a spiritual event for men and women separately, which began Friday night and ended Sunday afternoon. It was designed for the enrichment of a person's spiritual life based on the systematic doctrine of the church. The weekend was nondenominational and was for people of all faiths no matter where they were at in their own spiritual journeys. In the midst of this turmoil, these were wonderful prayer partners who sustained me while Nancy and I were apart for two months. Fortunately, I knew all of the criteria of a major depressive episode, and I fit every one. I sought out a wonderful psychiatrist who put me on medication and continued therapy with a local psychologist. Again, as time went on, I packed up our belongings in a big U-Haul truck and left for California the first of November in 1995. The journey from Traverse City to Upland, California, was a very therapeutic trip. I loved the drive; I took my time and was reunited with my beloved Nancy. Once I arrived in California, we rented a condo on a month-to-month basis. During that time, we looked for a new place to live and came upon a beautiful home in Alta Loma, California. Nancy liked the inside, and I liked the outside. We bought it and lived there to this day.

This is a picture of our home after our move to Spring Lake, Michigan. I just received my Doctorate of Ministry from Fuller Theological Seminary, Pasadena, California

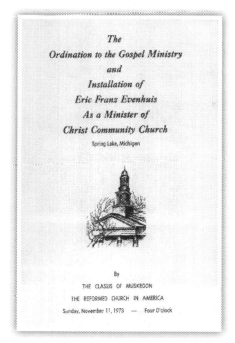

This is a picture of the bulletin on the occasion of my ordination

This is a picture of my continuing passion for sailing.

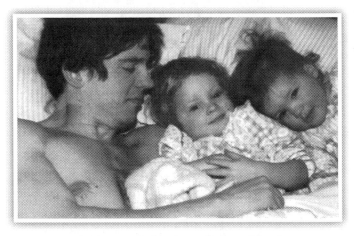

Me with Tera and Natalie as babies, Natalie was
born July 20, 1974 in Grand Haven, Michigan

Tera and Natalie in the pinafores
that Nancy made for them

This is a picture of Dr. Gary and Lois Voorman at my
70th birthday celebration. It was Dr. Voorman who
hired me to the hospital chaplain in California, 1978

This is the 36ft sailboat that Dr. Voorman purchased.
We were blessed with many wonderful family
outings on this boat (Natalie is on the boom)

Tera and Natalie in front of our Upland home on their
first day back to school at Ontario Christian High School

This was taken at our home on Mother's day, 1982.
This was the last day that we saw Dad alive

This is taken at Mom Evenhuis's home after dad's
death. John and Gayle flew in from Michigan
for dad's funeral in Redlands, California.

Dad also had a funeral in Holland,
Michigan. Dr Kromminga (to my right)
officiated at dad's funeral in Michigan

Nancy's sister, Peggy, married George Trindle. This
is photograph with their first child, Andrew.

George and Peggy Trindle, Ross,
Andrew, Ashley and Jessica

When we moved back to Traverse City, Michigan, we
also transported the 36 ft. Islander sailboat with us. (I
am the person wearing a hat) We sailed the boat from
Holland, Michigan to Traverse City in spring of 1994

This is a picture of me in front of Fellowship
Church in Traverse City, Michigan

This is a picture of the view from our
fabulous home on Old Mission Peninsula
overlooking the east bay of Lake Michigan

Two lovebirds enjoying our new home

This is a picture of Nancy and I, Nancy's mom
and dad, Tera and Natalie. We had many
wonderful family gatherings on our deck.

Tera and Marc de Falkenberg's wedding on
November 5, 1994 in Grand Rapids, Michigan

Our family at their wedding

Five

❧❧

The Exceptional Years

M oving back to California was the beginning of many blessings for Nancy, me, and our family. Not all the events were peaceful, nor was the road littered with rose petals, but they were very good years. I returned to California at age forty-nine. So, our exceptional years began.

The first thing I did was contact our good friends to enlist their help to move. Their response was, "Oh no, not again!" So we rented the biggest U-Haul we could find and moved all our belongings into our new home. Even though there was great reluctance for this hard physical task, all our friends were there to help. By nighttime all the beds were set up, and the kitchen unpacked and organized. The lesson learned here is that life, without friends, becomes very difficult and lonely. We thank God for these friendships that have lasted a lifetime.

STARTING OVER

It is not easy to start a practice again, so I worked part time as a hospice chaplain in downtown LA. Every day, I took the Metrolink train into

LA, where I had rented a parking space for my old turquoise-and-white truck. I visited patients in the LA -area and returned home in the evening on the train. Since Nancy worked full time at City of Hope, it relieved a lot of pressure for me. As I will tell you shortly, I left hospice to start up my own practice in Alta Loma. Building my practice and working for hospice was a two-year process.

During this period of time, two major events happened. The first event was when Dr. Roger Morgan invited me to become certified as a Parent Project presenter. Dr. Morgan was a very good friend when I was working at Horizon Hospital. He invited me to a weekend training workshop at Pepperdine University, overlooking the Pacific Ocean in Malibu, California. This training opened up a whole new world for my private practice.

My love for teenagers and their families was a pleasant surprise in my work. Teenagers were alive, vibrant, wild, and disrespectful. The Parent Project offered practical tools and hope for many families in distress. At the same time, I was working with families who were dealing with death and dying. My hospice work was challenging until my brother John passed away in December 1997. I remember vividly coming home from a Christmas hospice party and receiving a call informing us that John had passed away of adult respiratory distress syndrome. The reason this is significant is that one day I was visiting a hospice patient with the same diagnosis. You may find this peculiar, but for me, it was a direct sign from God that I needed to leave the hospice chaplain ministry. I begin focusing on my pastoral counseling practice. The verse that resonated in my mind was from Jeremiah: "I know the plans I have for you to give you a future and a hope" (Jeremiah 29:11 NIV). Indeed, God richly blessed both Nancy's work at City of Hope and my private practice.

Rose Petals

The first rose petal on this marvelous road was our daughter Natalie. She graduated from Calvin College with her BSN. She was also making plans to marry her fiancé, Mark Lodewyk. The wedding was planned for August 1997. Natalie moved back home earlier that year. While in Michigan, she took her nursing boards and failed. In Michigan, if you fail, you get a big envelope with instructions on how to reapply for the exam. When Natalie came to California, Nancy suggested she take a preparatory class before taking the nursing board exam again, which she did. She took the test and waited for the results.

One day, she went to get the mail. She came into the garage where I was working. Nancy was not home. Natalie came into the garage, crying, and carrying a big envelope. She said, "I didn't make it again."

As I was hugging her and holding the envelope, I noticed it read Do Not Bend.. I said, "Natalie, why would it say 'Do Not Bend' if you failed?"

We opened the envelope, and indeed, she had passed. She was now a licensed registered nurse. Her despondency turned into complete joy in two seconds. It was one of those wonderful moments that neither one of us will ever forget. Natalie started working at Huntington Memorial Hospital in Pasadena.

Things were going very well, and the plans for the wedding were taking shape. I thought that the wedding was spectacular. Mark's father, Robert Lodewyk, was a well-respected missionary in Nigeria. They made a special trip to the United States from Nigeria to attend the wedding. They brought with them handcarved wedding favors of men and women working. It was a special touch at the reception. Natalie was the most beautiful bride. When I walked her down the aisle, Robert asked me, "Who gives this woman to this man?" I responded, "Her mother and I do." Mark was so enthralled with her beauty that he was just staring at her. He didn't come to meet us and escort her to the altar. Robert said loudly, "Mark!" and then Mark remembered to come get Natalie. After this, I stepped forward and performed the marriage ceremony. Robert also participated in the ceremony. Mark's sisters-in-law played violin and piano. Mark's nieces and Natalie's cousins were flower girls. Austin was only two, but was the ring bearer. Following the ceremony, instead of throwing rice, we rented basketballs. We all threw them over Mark and Natalie like an arch as they left the church. They rode to our home for the reception in an antique car provided by Mike Fornier. The wedding reception was held in our backyard. The backyard was perfectly trimmed and mowed. There were nearly two hundred guests. The event was catered by Five Star Catering. The evening warmth was a blessing. The guests enjoyed the night and stayed late.

FAYE's DEATH

After this happy event, storm clouds were on the horizon again. We received a call from my niece Ruth, stating that Faye was very ill. She needed to go to the hospital. Faye had a reoccurring condition of congestive heart failure. It was not unusual for Faye to go to the hospital, but it turned out that this was to be her last visit. I flew to Michigan after John's wife, Gayle, notified me that Mom would need my attentions. She also asked me to help John, who was recovering from his lung cancer treatments. He was suffering from fatigue. Gayle had been a responsible caregiver to both Faye and John.

Now she needed to go see her daughter, Sue, in Massachusetts. John and I received conflicting information about Mom's condition. Her MD said she would probably be fine, but the nurses said she was dying. The doctor suggested she have a psychiatric evaluation. A psychiatrist came to see Mom. She was quite upset about this. Of course, she blamed me for this test being ordered. I had no part in the decision. Personally, I did not see any benefit to the evaluation, as she clearly was very ill. So I called Nancy and said, "Maybe it is best for you to fly out, if you want to visit Faye before she dies."

I picked Nancy up from the airport in Grand Rapids. We stopped to get some soup. Nancy was anxious to get to the hospital. But to my surprise, Mom passed away before Nancy and I arrived at the hospital. I wasn't expecting her death so suddenly. My daughter, Tera, and my oldest niece, Ruth, were at the hospital when Faye passed. It should be noted that Mom died on November 5, 1997. I find God's timing to be quite mysterious. This is also the date of Tera and Marc's wedding anniversary. I find it remarkable that they were willing to spend their anniversary visiting their grandmother on the day of her death.

Mom had worked for several years in Redlands, California, at Emmerson-Bartlett Funeral home. She helped people plan for their funeral services. She also was very organized for her own funeral. Her funeral was held at Yntema Funeral Home. She was buried next to Dad in the Holland Memorial Cemetery.

BROTHER JOHN'S DEATH

In early December, not long after Mom's death and burial, we were informed of John's untimely death. Over the past few years, John and I became very close. John always accepted me as his brother. He showed me great brotherly love though as a fact, we were cousins. In his earlier years, John struggled with addiction. I believe I played a significant part in his recovery from alcoholism. I directed him to the alcohol recovery program at St. Joseph's Hospital in Orange, California. John was a faithful and consistent member of the AA community for over twenty years. I remember vividly at his funeral where two AA members eulogized his life. Both Nancy and I were amazed and awed by the many people that John helped to recovery from their addictions. He was truly a great man. I still miss him to this day. We had many fond memories together. It's important to share that his wife, Gayle, is doing well, and lives in Zeeland, Michigan. Every year, we connect with Gayle and her family. I am very happy that this connection continues to be such a loving relationship.

NEW ROSE PETALS ON THE PATH: GRANDCHILDREN

The rose petals continued to fall upon our path when Marc, Tera, Austin, and Kaylee moved to California in 1999. We were very happy to have the de Falkenberg family in Southern California and living nearby.

Our first grandchild is Austin de Falkenberg, born May 9, 1995.

Our second grandchild is Kaylee de Falkenberg, born August 14, 1996.

Our third grandchild is Mariah Lynn Lodewyk on March 10, 2001.

Our fourth grandchild is Benjamin Marc de Falkenberg, born on March 28, 2001.

Our fifth grandchild is Marcus de Falkenberg, born on January 10, 2003.

Our sixth grandchild is Jenna de Falkenberg, born on February 12, 2004.

Our seventh grandchild is Noah Eric Lodewyk, born on May 28, 2004.

We now have our "Seven Wonders of the World". And I now have my perfect football team, which I always wanted. There are thirteen of us when we all get together. Thirteen precious lives. Nancy and I are the head coaches. These seven grandchildren have given Nancy and me great joy. We give thanks to God for seven healthy and beautiful grandchildren. One of my greatest joys was that I was able to baptize each and every one. I also pray that each of them will be filled with the Holy Spirit their whole lives, and without any doubt, I know that God has divine designs and plans for each of them. They are all amazing kids.

TERA AND NATALIE

Our daughter Tera is best known as "Mother Earth." She turned her strong will into becoming an amazing speech therapist. She received her master's degree from Cal State—LA. I admire her for her ability to finish what she started. Being both a mother and a student in a master's degree program is no easy task. Today, she is a full-time speech therapist at Winrose Elementary School in Rancho Cucamonga. She has her own private practice and is an adjunct professor at Cal Baptist University. But her best and most excellent quality is her deep love for children. She has made a profound difference in many children's lives.

Natalie Joy is truly a joy. Her name fits her well. She has an easygoing personality that has served her well as a wife, mother, and nurse. Natalie has also achieved her master's degree in nursing from San Jose State University, California. Her degree has allowed her to move into administrative positions in nursing. She is now a registered nurse at San Jose Kaiser hospital in California.

SONS-IN-LAW

Their fathers are also amazing. Mark Lodewyk's father and mother were missionaries in Nigeria. Mark is the youngest of four boys, and he was born in Nigeria. Mark is now the principal of Valley Christian High School in San Jose. Even though this is a prestigious position, it is fraught with many challenges. He has many wonderful qualities, but his best qualities are that he's a good husband to our daughter and a devoted father to our grandchildren. Marc de Falkenberg was born and raised in Chicago, Illinois. His parents are Robert and Joan. Robert was an executive at McDonald's Corporation, as a translator for the Latin American countries. Marc also went to Calvin College where he met our daughter, Tera. When he was at Calvin, he majored in recreation therapy. Marc also has many great qualities, but his best qualities are being a good husband to our daughter and a great father to our grandchildren. Every family needs a fun uncle like Uncle Mark! I am so grateful for their dedication to our family.

Because of our family, I've entitled this chapter "The Exceptional Years." Even though these were exceptional times, we experienced sad and difficult times, mingled with many happy occasions with the Marriott. We were invited to spend six days and five nights in Kauai, Hawaii, at a beautiful Marriott resort. But we were also expected to attend a presentation to purchase a time-share on the new resort on Oahu at Ko Olina Resort.

We said we weren't going to buy anything. Scott Coffee was our presenter. We were expecting a high-pressure salesman. He offered no pressure whatsoever. He said the time-share sells itself. He told us the terms, and we bought it. This purchase turned out to be a very good thing, and our families have spent many wonderful vacations at the beautiful Ko Olina resort. Shortly after our purchase at Ko Olina, we were invited to Marriott Newport Coast Villas. This time-share appealed to us, because it was only fifty miles away from Alta Loma. This also proved to be a very wise purchase, and our families have experienced many wonderful vacations together at this beautiful property.

The highlight for me at Newport was "Campa Grandpa." I lined up all seven kids in a row from oldest to youngest. I told them they had to follow the rules of Campa Grandpa, which meant, "*No* whining, complaining, arguing, or quitting!" I prepared various activities around the property. They included rolling a basketball down the long stairs and running back up with the ball, shooting basketballs, and putting on an artificial green. There were great fountains to run around. I included calisthenics. Campa Grandpa ended with a swimming pool contest. Prizes were given to everyone. All seven grandchildren completed the course. Their final reward was a trip to a Newport bakery for delicious donuts. All the kids came back happy, singing the praises of Grandpa. We still enjoy our time-share with the family to this day.

Papa Watson's Death (Warren)

Storm clouds were on the horizon once again. This time, it was the issue with Grandpa Watson's health. In 2002, Dad Watson suffered a severe stroke. He was eighty-two years old. When this occurred, Mom Watson called. She said the doctor told her to call her children home. So Peggy and Nancy flew to Minnesota. Kathy and Mike

House, Nancy's cousins, were at the airport to take the girls the 120 miles trip to the hospital in Olivia. Dad Watson was still alive, but clearly very impaired with paralysis on his left side and speech impairment. The following day he was transported to Minneapolis to Northwestern Hospital. After a long hospital stay, he needed further nursing care. He was transferred to the Renvilla Nursing Home. Part of his rehabilitation was speech therapy. I arrived to visit, and when he saw me he said, spelled out with great deliberation, "E-V-E-N-H-U-I-S." His mind and his sense of humor were still sharp. I wonder to this day, if that inspired Tera in her work.

In December, Peggy took her mom and dad to their home in Arizona. There he was able to participate in church activities. He visited with friends, but on a limited basis. His ability to be fully engaged was diminished. It was sad to see a very strong man with a lot of vitality become weak and frail. I was able to say goodbye to Dad Watson when he was at the Arizona Heart Institute. Though Dad was not much of a hugger, George Trindle and I both were able to give him a hug and a kiss goodbye. Nancy and Peggy stayed on with Mom.

One night, after visiting Dad in the hospital, Mom and Nancy were driving back to their home in Sun City. It was late on a dark night when a truck passed them. He was driving very erratically. Nancy was driving cautiously. Two small, expensive sports cars also passed their vehicle going at a high rate of speed. Soon, Nancy and Mom saw the truck also starting to race with these cars. Then he quickly lost control and spun off the freeway into the median. There was a lot of dust surrounding the truck. Then they saw two vehicles on the opposite side of the freeway. They were also out of control.

Suddenly a vehicle crossed through the median with a sheared-off top of the car. Nancy thought it was a convertible. She wondered why it could go so fast, when it appeared that no one was in the car. Nancy called the police to report what she had witnessed. She was sure people died that night. Nancy knew her dad was not doing well, and this verse came to her, "Yea though I walk through the valley of the shadow of death I will fear no evil for thou art with me."

As I reflect on this event, I can clearly see that Nancy and her mother were protected by angels. As terrible as that accident was, it could have taken their lives.

In summary, Dad was transferred from the hospital to hospice care for a short time. He passed away there peacefully. His body was flown back to Minnesota. I had the honor of conducting his funeral. It was a bittersweet time as spring was so beautiful. Dad loved his Minnesota farm.

Dad always ended his prayers with this phrase, "We ask all these things pleading on the merits of our Lord and Savior, Jesus Christ." So I dug into my Berkhof systematic theology book. I wanted to know more about the merits of our Lord and Savior, Jesus Christ. The answer was that the merits of our Lord Jesus Christ are found in the state of humiliation and the state of exaltation. The Bible says it is appointed once for man to die. Dad's appointment was not too soon and not too late. He lived a good and healthy life. He loved the land. He was a hardworking man. He was a quiet and humble man. He was well-respected in his community. It was only appropriate that on the day of his funeral, there was a quiet and gentle rain. The earth that he loved so much was happy for the rain.

Mom Watson missed Dad very, very much. She carried on as best she could. After being married nearly sixty years, life without your spouse is very lonely. Following Dad's death, Mom sold the home place. Eventually, Mom bought a double-wide mobile home. She lived in Upland every summer until 2007. Mom spent her winters in her home in her Sun City, Arizona. It was always a happy time to return to Arizona. She resumed her golfing and activities at West Valley Christian Fellowship.

The year 2007 was not an easy one for Mom. She had autonomic nervous system failure, which slowly limited her activities. She often had spells where she fainted. One day while I was working at home, I got a phone call. She said she fell. I dropped everything and drove to her home. She had fallen outside, but she was already resting on her bed when I arrived.

I sat next to her. I took her pulse, and then said, "I have no idea why I am doing this, but it makes me feel better." We both had a good laugh over that! I took her back to our home for the day. The Monday before Thanksgiving, she spent with Peggy. Tuesday morning she had a dental appointment. Nancy called her to go shopping for groceries for Thanksgiving. But Mom did not answer the phone. Nancy called Peggy to check on her. Peggy and George went over to her home. When they entered the house, they found her lying in the bed as if she were sleeping peacefully.

Sadly, she was dead. They notified the police. Soon Nancy was able to join them. The mortician was called to pick up her body. Because she died two days before Thanksgiving, we needed to plan and move quickly. Funeral arrangements were made to fly her body to Minnesota. On Thanksgiving Day, the whole family flew to Minnesota. When we arrived late at night we were all hungry, sad, and tired. No restaurants were open except for IHOP. After we ate, we drove to Renville, Minnesota.

The next morning, Nancy and Peggy went to the funeral home to make the final arrangements. Once again, I was honored to officiate at her funeral. She liked a sermon I had preached at Bethel Christian Reformed Church in Sun Valley, California. Mom always liked to go to that church. I had preached on the Providence of God. I knew Mom wanted me to preach that sermon. My favorite catechism question is, "What do you believe about the providence of God?" Without reviewing the entire sermon, I can say, "All things come to us not by fate, but by our Father's loving hand."

Renville was where Mom spent most of her life. She was well-respected by everyone. And her funeral was extremely large, and the church was packed. Mom's death was an end of an era. I had a great respect and love for her. She truly loved me more than just a son-in-law.

Following Mom's death, the question Nancy and Peggy needed to answer was what to do with the land. Our initial plan was to keep it. We would continue renting to Curtis Watson. Mom was already in a rental agreement with Curt. It is important to note that Curtis was Nancy and Peggy's cousin, the son of Deane and Grace Watson. Curt was a partner with his father and Dad Watson for a short time.

After Deane's death, he had been Dad Watson's partner until Dad's retirement. Curtis was a big farmer in the Renville area and very involved in land management, custom cultivating, and harvesting. He was involved in politics as it related to agriculture. He was a visionary, and so we decided that the land should be rented to Curt. This turned out to be a very positive experience for us all for many years. Curt and his wife, Janel, would also rent Mom's Arizona house in the winter months.

It was during these times that George, Peggy, Nancy, and I would visit them in Arizona. There we would golf, and enjoy our time together. Our last visit with Curt was March 2012. We arrived on Thursday, March 9. We had a wonderful time visiting, playing golf, and enjoying the lovely weather. On Saturday, March 11, Curt, myself, and two other friends played golf. Everything seemed fine. We went out for dinner after. Nancy had a meaningful and spiritual conversation with Curt. They talked about how blessed they were to grow up in Christian homes. It was evident that over the last few years Curt's faith had become more mature and meaningful to him. There was a true change in his entrepreneur style. He was mindful that he wanted to pass on the farm to the fourth generation, his two sons Eric and Aaron. Early Sunday morning, approximately 4:00 a.m., Janel frantically aroused us. She said, "I can't wake Curt." We called 911 and were instructed to begin CPR, which Nancy had already begun. The ambulance and sheriff came quickly. The medical personnel took over doing CPR. Nancy did a wonderful job of attempting to revive Curtis. He was transported to the hospital, where we had to wait. I vividly remember sitting in the hospital's private waiting room. The doctor came in, and said in a sad voice that they were unable to revive Curtis. This event shocked me to the bone. It was completely unexpected. He was only sixty-three years old.

I was once again honored to officiate at Curt's funeral. I'm not one to use a funeral to present the gospel. However, I felt led to do so at Curt's funeral. My theme was walking with God is the best walk. That's exactly what I said at his funeral. Just as I concluded the sermon, a train passed through Renville, and the haunting sound of the train whistle penetrated the service. It was truly a God moment. On the way to the gravesite, we passed by Curtis's farm. All of the farm equipment, tractors, plows, and sprayers, were all lined up along the road. It was a fitting tribute. Even his faithful dog was lined up, as if at attention. Another man who loved the land was gone.

Curt's death made us think differently about the land. Nancy and I visited a wise farm realtor and discussed our future. He said, "Eventually, the farm will be sold if no one in the family wants to farm it. There will be succession." We discussed the matter with George and Peggy. We all agreed that the best solution was to sell the land. We made a contract with a local farm realtor, Eldon Krull. Slowly, piece by piece, all the farm land was sold.

Dad Watson had said, "Don't sell the farm." Well, we didn't listen to his advice. His words haunted both Peggy, and Nancy for a long time. Selling the farm was not easy, and it signaled the end of an era that can never be recaptured.

In reality, this really does end the exceptional years that we have lived since we moved back to California in 1995. It is now 2020, twenty-five years that we have returned to live in California. I can truly say that these twenty-five years have been exceptional years. I remember Dad Watson's song that he wrote shortly before his death, "How Blessed We Are, How Blessed We Are." How true it is that throughout our life's journey how blessed we are.

Mark and Natalie's wedding August 2, 1997

The most happy family: Tera, Natalie, Nancy and me

Natalie and I are ready to walk down the aisle

Faye died November 5, 1997

Brother John died December 1997

The last photo of Mom and Dad Watson. Dad
died April 2003, Mom died November 2007

Curtis Watson (Nancy's cousin) died March 2012.
Photo with Curt and Janel with Uncle Bill Watson

A great blessing for me was to baptize all seven
grandchildren. Mariah Lynn Lodewyk's baptism

Marcus Robert Lodewyk's baptism

Benjamin Marc de Falkenberg's baptism
with Pastor Tim Spykstra and me

Jenna Natalie de Falkenberg's baptism

Marc and Tera de Falkenberg's family:
Kaylee, Benjamin, Jenna and Austin

Mark and Natalie Lodewyk's family:
Mariah, Marcus and Noah

Campa Grandpa and the grandchildren

The seven wonders of the world: Jenna, Marcus,
Kaylee, Austin, Mariah, Benjamin and Noah

This is a photograph at my seventieth birthday honoring
Nancy's sister, Peggy, and her husband George Trindle

George and Peggy Trindle's family:
Ross, Jessica, Ashley and Andrew

Conclusion

The Circle of Trust

Edward R. Morrow was a newscaster who ended every evening newscast with these words, "Good night and good luck." Every time I hear the word *luck*, I replace it with question and answer twenty-seven of Heidelberg Catechism. The question is, "What do you understand by the providence of God? Providence is the almighty and ever-present power of God, by which he upholds, as with his Hand, Heaven, Earth and all creatures. And so rules them that leaf and blade, rain and drought, fruitful and lean years, food and drink, health and sickness, prosperity and poverty, all things, in fact, come to us not by chance, but from His fatherly hand." As you have read in these previous pages, my whole life was and is a story of God's providential grace. Sometimes, this truth is a hard pill to swallow. But it is true.

It's no mystery to anyone that I have always been an adventurer, and a wanderer. When I was a kid, my favorite song was "The Wayward Wind." There is within me a restlessness. Sailing has always been a cure for my wanderlust. Paul Tournier wrote a book called *The Adventure of Living*. I now look back on my life as a great adventure. The value of adventure is that you get to enter into your next adventure. My best adventure is that I entered into an intimate relationship with God. God, through my amazing adventure, has made me the person that I was created to be. When my life is over, my adventure will continue. I think about Joshua, in the Old Testament. Joshua was entering into his own adventure of crossing the Jordan River. Before he crossed the river, he asked the people of Israel, "If serving the Lord seems undesirable to you, then choose for yourself this day who you will serve. But as for me and my household, we will serve the Lord" (Joshua 24:15 NIV).

I like the Israelite's response. They said, "Far be it from us to forsake the Lord to serve other gods. It was the Lord our God himself who brought us out of Egypt from the land of slavery, and performed those great signs before our eyes. He protected us on our entire journey through which we have traveled. We too will serve the Lord, because he is our God" (Joshua 24:16–18 NIV).

And so the end of the matter is that Little Ricky has been enveloped in God's wonderful Circle of Trust. He was in that Circle of Trust from the very moment of conception and will be to his very last breath on this earth. After reading this book, I hope that the one major theme that you can bring home is Psalm 121: "The Lord is your keeper. He will watch over your whole life. The Lord will watch over your coming and going both now and forevermore" (Psalm 121:7 NIV).

I have had many keepers in my life. My mother Evelyn chose to keep me. I was close to being aborted. The good doctor did not want an abortion. Jim Schilstra kept me by giving me up, the Walters kept me by taking me in, Robert and Faye kept me by adopting me. Reverend Jim Kok kept me by being the best friend ever. The good doctor Gary Voorman kept me by sending me to California. Of course, there were many others, but the greatest of these keepers has to be Nancy. As Joshua said, "God has performed great signs before my very own eyes, has protected me on my entire journey through which I have traveled". And now I will forever lean on the everlasting arms of Jesus.

Enjoy your Circle of Trust. We all have one.

Little Ricky is still little Ricky and is
ready for his next adventure.

This is a very handsome picture of my friend Nathan
Little. Without Nathan's thoughtful and keen mind
this book would have never been launched. Seriously,
Nathan has been the rocket fuel for the publication
of this book. I will also add that Nathan is a rocket
scientist at a premier aerospace company.

Printed in the United States
By Bookmasters